PLAYSCRIPT 112

WOMEN BEWARE WOMEN

(With Thomas Middleton)

PITY IN HISTORY

Howard Barker

JOHN CALDER : LONDON
RIVERRUN PRESS : NEW YORK

This edition first published in Great Britain, 1989, by
John Calder (Publishers) Ltd
18 Brewer Street, London W1R 4AS

and in the United States of America, 1989, by
Riverrun Press Inc
1170 Broadway, New York, NY 10001

Women Beware Women first published in 1986 in London and New
York by John Calder (Publishers) Ltd and Riverrun Press Inc.
Pity in History first published in *Gambit International Theatre
Review*, No. 41 by John Calder (Publishers) Ltd, London, 1984.

British Library Cataloguing in Publication Data
Middleton, Thomas
  Women beware women.
  I. Title   II. Barker, Howard   III. Barker,
  Howard. Pity in history.
  822′.3   PR2714.W6

  ISBN 0-7145-4134-6

Library of Congress Cataloging-in-Publication Data
Middleton, Thomas, d.1627.
  Women beware women
  1. Great Britain—History—Civil War, 1642–1649—
Drama.   I. Barker, Howard.   II. Barker, Howard.
Pity in history.   1987.   III. Title.
PR6052.A6485A6   1987   822′.3   87-4477

ISBN 0-7145-4134-6

Typeset in 10/11pt Times British by Gilbert Composing Services,
Leighton Buzzard, Bedfordshire.
Printed in Great Britain by Hillman Printers, (Frome) Ltd, Somerset

They call me a pessimist, but I only have a sense of impossibility. Middleton's pessimism is a pessimism of the soul.

His lack of hope brought out the humanist in me.

Florence. England. The super-finance economies. And I discover in him the man who knows love also is a commodity.

The body as currency. Innocence pays no dividends. The orgasm is the deal.

Even the lowest clerk is taught to hoard. So Leantio hoards Bianca. The flesh however, cannot be held. It is not stable, any more than money.

My characters have a terrible consistency. Middleton exclaims even the mother's love has got its price.

Middleton's world is a sexual stock exchange. And I redeem his lost souls, I, the pessimist, redeem his rotted kindness.

Middleton says the woman marries a fool and fucks her favourite. I say no one is as stupid as they appear.

Middleton says a woman buys her sex. I say even bought sex carries hope.

Middleton says lust leads to the grave. I say desire alters perception.

He saw the comedy in cruelty. He knew women were not better than men, and that we collaborate in our oppression. He knew girls were ruthless also.

But his morality was false. His cardinal is a lie, and a spokesman for a lie. So I remade the cardinal. When morality is only convention, you get bad art.

The Left has ignored the body. It has yielded sexuality to the reactionaries. Middleton knew the body was the source of politics. He did not know it was also the source of hope.

Our socialism must eschew the cardinals.

This version of *Women Beware Women* was first performed at The Royal Court Theatre, London, on 1st February 1986, with the following cast:

LEANTIO A Factor	STEVAN RIMKUS
BIANCA His Wife	JOANNE WHALLEY
THE WIDOW His Mother	ELIZABETH BRADLEY
GUARDIANO Uncle to the Ward	PETER SPROULE
FABRITIO Father to Isabella	NORMAN HENRY
LIVIA His Sister	MAGGIE STEED
ISABELLA His Daughter	MELANIE HILL
HIPPOLITO Her Uncle	COLIN McCORMACK
WARD A rich young heir	SIMON RUSSELL BEALE
SORDIDO His Man	GARY OLDMAN
DUKE OF FLORENCE	NIGEL DAVENPORT
LORD CARDINAL His Brother	NORMAN HENRY
Music performed by	JULIAN BREWER, NICHOLAS BRIGGS, PAUL EDLIN, ROBERT FARLEY, WILLIAM O'SULLIVAN
Directed by	WILLIAM GASKILL
Designed by	KANDIS COOK

Women Beware Women was first performed in the United States of America at Playhouse 91, New York, on 8 March 1987 with the following cast:

LEANTIO	NEIL MAFFIN
BIANCA	CAROLINE BECK
THE WIDOW	FLORENCE WINSTON
GUARDIANO	JOHN HEFFERNAN
FABRITIO	MARCUS POWELL
LIVIA	SALLY KIRKLAND
ISABELLA	KATELL PLEVEN
HIPPOLITO	ROY STEINBERG
WARD	BARRY JON LYNCH
SORDIDO	JUDSON CAMP
DUKE OF FLORENCE	CHET LONDON
LORD CARDINAL	WILLIAM NEWMAN
Directed by	SHARON GANS
Designed by	WOLFGANG ROTH

The Scene
FLORENCE

PART ONE

Scene One

LEANTIO *with* BIANCA *and* MOTHER.

MOTHER: Thy sight was never yet more precious to me!
Welcome, with all the affection of a mother, that comfort can
express from natural love! Since thy birth joy, thou wast not
more dear to me than this hour presents thee to my heart!

LEANTIO: Alas, poor affectionate soul, how her joys speak to
me! I have observed it often, and I know it is the fortune
commonly of knavish children to have the loving'st mothers.

MOTHER: What's this gentlewoman?

LEANTIO: Oh, you have named the most undervalued'st
purchase, that youth of man had ever knowledge of! As
often as I look upon that treasure, and know it to be mine, it
joys me that I ever was ordained to have a being, and to live
amongst men! I must confess I am guilty of one sin, mother,
more than I brought into the world with me; but that I glory
in; 'tis theft, but noble as ever greatness yet shot up withal.

MOTHER: How's that?

LEANTIO: Never to be repented, mother, though sin be
death! Do you now behold her! Look on her well, she's mine:
look on her better! Now, say, if it be not the best piece of
theft that ever was committed. And I have my pardon for it.
'Tis sealed from Heaven by marriage.

MOTHER: Married to her!

LEANTIO: You must keep council, mother, I am undone else.
If it be known, I have lost her. From Venice her consent and I
have brought her, from parents great in wealth, more now in
rage; but let storms spend their furies. Now we have got a
shelter over our quiet innocent loves, we are contented.
Little money she has brought me, view but her face, you may

see all her dowry, save that which lies locked up in hidden virtues, like jewels kept in cabinets.

MOTHER: You know not what you have done. What ableness have you to·do her right, in maintenance fitting her birth and virtues, which every woman of necessity looks for, and most to go above it, not confined by their conditions, bloods or births, but flowing to affections, wills and humours?

LEANTIO: Speak low, sweet mother; you are able to spoil as many as come within the hearing. I pray do not you teach her to rebel, when she's in a good way to obedience. I'll prove an excellent husband— here's my hand—lay in provision, follow my business roundly, and make you a grandmother in forty weeks! Go, pray salute her, bid her welcome cheerfully.

MOTHER: Gentlewoman, thus much is a debt of courtesy. *(She kisses* BIANCA.*)* And now, salute you by the name of daughter, which may challenge more than ordinary respect. *(She kisses her again.)*

BIANCA: Well, this is well now, and I think few mothers of three score will mend it.

MOTHER: What I can bid you welcome to is mean; but make it all you own. We are full of wants and cannot welcome worth.

LEANTIO: Now this is scurvy! These old folks talk of nothing but defects, because they grow so full of them themselves!

BIANCA: Kind mother, there is nothing can be wanting to her that does enjoy all her desires. I have forsook friends, fortunes, and my country, and hourly I rejoice in it. I'll call this place the place of my birth now—and rightly, too, for here my love was born, and that's the birthday of a woman's joy. *(To* LEANTIO.*)* You have not bid me welcome since I came...

LEANTIO: That I did, questionless.

BIANCA: No sure, how was it? I have quite forgot it.

LEANTIO: Thus. *(He kisses her.)*

BIANCA: Oh, sir, 'tis true, now I remember well; I have done thee wrong, pray take it again, sir. *(She kisses him.)*

LEANTIO: How many of these wrongs could I put up with in an hour? and turn up the glass for twice as many more!

BIANCA: Thanks, sweet mother; the voice of her that bore me is not more pleasing. *(They go in.)*

LEANTIO: Though my own care and my rich master's trust lay their commands both on my factorship, this day and

night I'll know no other business but her and her dear
welcome. It is a bitterness to think upon tomorrow, that I
must leave her still to the sweet hopes of the week's end. Oh,
melancholy Florence! Didst thou but know what a most
matchless jewel thou art now mistress of, a pride would
take thee able to shoot destruction through the bonds of all
thy youthful sons! But 'tis great policy to keep choice
treasures in obscurest places; should we show thieves our
wealth 'twould make them bolder. The jewel is cased up
from all men's eyes; who could imagine now a gem were
kept, of that great value, under this plain roof? Old mothers
know the world, and such as these, when sons lock chests,
are good to look to keys.

Scene Two

GUARDIANO, FABRITIO, LIVIA.

GUARDIANO: Has your daughter seen him yet?

FABRITIO: No matter, she shall love him.

GUARDIANO: Nay, let's have fair play! He has been now my
    ward some fifteen year, and it is my purpose, as time calls
    upon me, to tender him a wife. Now, sir, this wife I'd fain
    elect out of a daughter of yours. You see, my meaning's fair.
    If now this daughter, so tendered, should offer to refuse
    him—

FABRITIO: I still say she shall love him.

GUARDIANO: Yet again? And shall she have no reason for
    this love?

FABRITIO: Why, do you think that women love with reason?
    I had a wife. She ran mad for me. She had no reason for it
    aught I could perceive. What do you think, lady sister?
    You're an experienced widow.

LIVIA: I must offend you, then, if truth will do it, and take my
    niece's part, and call it injustice to force her love to one she
    never saw. Maids should both see and like—all little enough.
    If they love truly after that, 'tis well. She takes one man till
    death, that's a hard task, I tell you.

FABRITIO: Why, is not man tied to the same observance,
    lady sister, and in one woman?

LIVIA: 'Tis enough for him. Besides, he tastes of many dishes that we poor wretches never lay our lips to—as obedience, subjection, duty and such kickshaws, all of our making, but served into them; and if we lick a finger then, sometimes, we are not to blame. Your best cooks use it.

FABRITIO: Thou art a sweet lady, sister, and a witty.

LIVIA: A witty! Oh, the bud of commendation, fit for a girl of sixteen! I am blown, man! I should be wise by this time. I have buried my two husbands in good fashion, and never mean more to marry.

GUARDIANO: No, why so, lady?

LIVIA: Because the third shall never bury me. I think I am more than witty. How think you, sir?

FABRITIO: I have often paid fees to a counsellor had a weaker brain.

LIVIA: Then I must tell you, your money was soon parted. Where is my niece? If you have any hope 'twill prove a wedding, 'tis fit she should have one sight of him.

FABRITIO: Look out her uncle, and you are sure of her. Those two are never asunder. They've been heard in argument at midnight, moonshine nights are noondays with them, they walk out their sleeps. They're like a chain, draw but one link, all follows.

HIPPOLITO, ISABELLA *enter.*

GUARDIANO: Oh affinity, what piece of excellent workmanship art thou? It's work clean wrought, for there's no lust but love in it, and that abundantly, when in stranger things, there is no love at all but what lust brings...

FABRITIO (*to* ISABELLA). On with your mask, for it's your part to see now, and not be seen. See what you mean to like— nay, and I charge you—like what you see. Do you hear me? There's no dallying. The gentlemen's almost twenty, and it's time he was getting lawful heirs, and you abreeding on 'em.

ISABELLA: Good father!

FABRITIO: Tell me not of tongues and rumours! You'll say the gentleman is somewhat simple—the better for a husband, were you wise, for those that marry fools live ladies' lives. On with the mask, I'll hear no more. He's rich, the fool's hid under bushels.

LIVIA: Not so hid, neither, but here's a great foul piece of him, methinks, what will he be when he comes altogether?

Enter WARD *and* SORDIDO, *with trapsticks.*

WARD: Beat him? I beat him out the field with his own catstick, yet gave him the first hand!

SORDIDO: Oh, strange...!

WARD: I did it, then he set jacks on me.

SORDIDO: What, my lady's tailor?

WARD: Ay and I beat him, too!

SORDIDO: Nay, that's no wonder, he's used to beating...

WARD: I tickled him when I came once to my tippings!

SORDIDO: Now you talk on 'em, there was a poulterer's wife made a great complaint of you last night to your guardiner, that you struck a bump in her child's head as big as an egg!

WARD: An egg may prove a chicken, then in time the poulterer's wife will get by it. When I am in game I am furious; came my mother's eyes in my way I would not lose a fair end! No, were she alive with but one tooth in her head, I should venture the striking out of that! Coads me, my guardiner! Prithee lay up my cat and catstick safe!

GUARDIANO: Ward!

WARD: I feel myself after any exercise horribly prone... let me but ride, I'm lusty—a cock-horse straight, in faith!

GUARDIANO: Ward! I must new school you!

WARD: School me? I scorn that now, I am past schooling. I am not so base to learn to read and write, I was born to better fortunes in my cradle. (GUARDIANO, SORDIDO, WARD *go out.*)

FABRITIO: How do you like him, girl? This is your husband.

LIVIA: Oh, soft there, brother! Though you be a justice, your warrant cannot be served out of your territory. You may compel, out of the power of a father, things merely harsh to a maid's flesh and blood, but when you come to love, there the soil alters.

FABRITIO: Marry him she shall then; let her agree upon love afterwards. *(He goes out.* LIVIA *kisses* HIPPOLITO *on the cheek.)*

LIVIA: Prithee, cheer up thy niece with special counsel... *(She goes out.)*

HIPPOLITO: I would 'twere fit to speak to her what I would, but 'twas not a thing ordained, Heaven has forbid it. Feed inward, you my sorrows, make no noise; consume me silent, let me be stark dead ere the world know I'm sick...

ISABELLA: Marry a fool! Oh, the heartbreakings of miserable maids, where love's enforced! The best condition is but bad enough—when women have their choices, commonly they do but buy their thraldoms, and bring great portions to men to keep 'em in subjection. Men buy their slaves, but women buy their masters. What, are you sad too, uncle? 'Faith, then there's a whole household down together; where shall I seek my comfort now, when my best friend's distressed? What is it afflicts you sir?

HIPPOLITO: 'Faith, nothing but one grief that will not leave me.

ISABELLA: Oh, be cheered, sweet uncle, how long has it been upon you? I never spied it! How long, I pray, sir?

HIPPOLITO: Since I first saw you, niece, and left Bologna.

ISABELLA: And could you deal so unkindly with my heart, to keep it up so long hid from my pity?

HIPPOLITO: You of all creatures, niece, must never hear on it. 'Tis not a thing ordained for you to know.

ISABELLA: Not I, sir! All my joys that word cuts off! You made profession once you loved me best—'twas but profession!

HIPPOLITO: Yes, I do it truly, and fear I shall be chid for it. Know the worst, then. I love thee dearlier than an uncle can.

ISABELLA: Why, so you ever said, and I believed it!

HIPPOLITO: So simple is the goodness of her thoughts they understand not yet the unhallowed language of a sinner. I must be forced to come nearer. As a man loves his wife, so I love thee.

ISABELLA: What's that? Methought I heard ill news come towards me, which commonly we hear too soon. It shall never come so near mine ear again. Farewell all friendly solaces and discourses, I'll learn to live without ye, for your dangers are greater than your comforts! *(She goes out.)*

Scene Three

LEANTIO.

LEANTIO: Methinks I'm even as dull now at departure as men observe great gallants the next day after a revels; you shall see 'em look much of my fashion, if you mark 'em well.

'Tis even a second hell to part from pleasure when man has got a smack of it.

BIANCA *and* MOTHER *enter, above.*

I have no power to go now and I should be hanged. Farewell all business! I desire no more than I see yonder. Let the goods at quay look to themselves, why should I toil my youth out? Oh, fie, what a religion have I leaped into! Get out again, for shame! The man loves best when his care's most—that show his zeal to love. Good to make sport when the chest's full and the long warehouse cracks.

BIANCA: I perceive, sir, you are not gone yet. I have good hope you'll stay now.

LEANTIO: Farewell, I must not.

BIANCA: Come, come pray return. Tomorrow, adding but a little care more, will despatch all as well—believe me, it will, sir.

LEANTIO: I could well wish myself where you would have me; but love that's wanton must be ruled awhile by love that's careful, or all goes to ruin.

BIANCA: But this one night, I prithee...

LEANTIO: Alas, I'm in for twenty if I stay. Again, farewell to thee...

BIANCA: Since it must, farewell, too... *(He goes out.)*

MOTHER: 'Faith, daughter, you are to blame. You take the course to make him an ill husband, troth you do, and that disease is catching, I can tell you. What cause have you to weep? Would that I had no more, that have lived threescore years! His absence cannot last five days at utmost.

Enter applauding crowd.

BIANCA *(recovering).* What's the meaning of this hurry, can you tell, Mother?

MOTHER: What a memory I have! I see by that years come upon me. Why 'tis a yearly custom and solemnity, religiously observed by the duke and state to St Mark's Temple, the fifteenth of April. See if my dull brains had not quite forgot it! I would not be ten years younger again that you had lost the sight. Now you shall see our duke, a goodly gentleman of his years.

BIANCA: Is he old, then?

MOTHER: About fifty-five.
BIANCA: That's no great age in a man. He's then at best for wisdom and for judgement.
MOTHER: You shall behold all our chief states of Florence. Take this stool.

DUKE *enters, with* CARDINAL *and* HIPPOLITO.

DUKE *(to* CARDINAL). Brother, what is it commands your eye so powerfully? Speak, you seem lost!
CARDINAL: The thing I look on seems so. To my eyes lost forever.
DUKE: You look on me.
CARDINAL: What grief it is to a religious feeling to think a man should have a friend so goodly, so wise, so noble, nay, a duke, a brother, and all this certainly damned!
DUKE *(seeing* BIANCA, *stops, stares up).* How?
CARDINAL: 'Tis no wonder, if your great sin can do it. Dare you sleep, for fear of never waking but to death? And dedicate upon a strumpet's love the strength of your affections, zeal, and health? I shall show you how more unfortunate you stand in sin than the low private man. All his offences, like enclosed grounds, keep but about himself and seldom stretch his own soul's bounds, but great man, every sin thou commit'st shows like a flame upon a mountain, 'tis seen far about, and with a big wind made of popular breath, the sparkles fly through cities!
DUKE *(still gazing up).* If you have done, I have. No more, sweet brother...
CARDINAL: I know time spent in goodness is too tedious. How dare you venture on eternal pain that cannot bear a minute's reprehension? Oh, my brother, what were you, if you were taken now! Think upon it, brother! Can you come so near it for a fair strumpet's love, and fall into a torment that knows neither end nor bottom?
DUKE *(tearing his eyes away, looking to* CARDINAL). Brother of spotless honour, let me weep the first of my repentance on thy bosom, and show the blest fruits of a thankful spirit. And if I ever keep a woman more unlawfully, may I want penitence at my greatest need... *(The* CARDINAL *smiles with joy, kisses his hand. With a parting glance at* BIANCA, THE DUKE *moves on.)*
MOTHER: How like you, daughter?

BIANCA: Methinks my soul could dwell upon the reverence of such a solemn and most worthy custom. Did not the duke look up? Methought he saw us.

MOTHER: That's everyone's conceit that sees a duke!

BIANCA: Most likely so.

MOTHER: Come, come, we'll end this argument below!

Scene Four

HIPPOLITO, LIVIA.

LIVIA: A strange affection, brother, when I think on't! I wonder how thou camest by it.

HIPPOLITO: Even as easily as man comes by destruction, which oft-times he wears in his own bosom.

LIVIA: Is the world so populous in women, and creation so progidal in beauty and so various, yet does love turn thy point to thine own blood? 'Tis somewhat too unkindly. Must thy eye dwell evily on the fairness of thy kindred, and seek not where it should?

HIPPOLITO: Never was man's misery so soon sewed up.

LIVIA: Nay, I love you so, that I shall venture much to keep a change from you so fearful as this grief will bring upon you. Let not passion waste the goodness of thy time and of thy fortune. I can bring forth as pleasant fruits as sensuality wishes in all her teeming longings. This I can do.

HIPPOLITO: Oh, nothing that can make my wishes perfect ...

LIVIA: Sir, I could give as shrewd a lift to chastity as any she that wears a tongue in Florence. She'd need to be a good horsewoman and sit fast whom my strong argument could not fling at last.

HIPPOLITO: I am past hope.

LIVIA: You are not the first, brother, has attempted things more forbidden than this seems to be. Thou shalt see me do a strange cure as ever was wrought on a disease so mortal and near akin to shame. When shall you see her?

HIPPOLITO: Never in comfort more.

LIVIA: You're so impatient, too.

HIPPOLITO: Will you believe—'death, she has forsworn my company, and sealed it with a blush.

LIVIA: So, I perceive, all lies upon my hands, then. The more glory when the work's finished. *(She kisses him.)* Your absence, gentle brother. I must bestir my wits for you.

HIPPOLITO: Ay, to great purpose. *(He goes out.)*

LIVIA: I take a course to pity him so much now, that I have none left for modesty and myself. This 'tis to grow so liberal—you have few sisters that love their brother's ease above their own honesties. *(Enter* ISABELLA.*)* Niece, your love's welcome. Alas, what draws that paleness to thy cheeks? This enforced marriage?

ISABELLA: It helps, good aunt, amongst some other griefs.

LIVIA: Indeed, the ward is simple.

ISABELLA: Simple! That were well! Why, one might make good shift with such a husband. But he's a fool entailed, he halts downright in it.

LIVIA: And knowing this, I hope 'tis at your choice to take or refuse, niece.

ISABELLA: You see it is not. I loathe him more than beauty can hate death.

LIVIA: Let it appear, then.

ISABELLA: How can I, being born with that obedience that must submit unto a father's will?

LIVIA: Be not offended, prithee, if I set by the name of niece awhile, and bring in pity in a stranger fashion. It lies here in this breast, would cross this match.

ISABELLA: How, cross it, aunt?

LIVIA: Ay, and give thee more liberty than thou hast reason yet to apprehend.

ISABELLA: Sweet aunt, in goodness keep not hid from me what may befriend my life.

LIVIA: Yes, yes, I must when I return to reputation, and think upon the solemn vow I made to your dead mother, my most loving sister... 'twas a secret I have took special care of, delivered by your mother on her deathbed—that's nine years now, and I'll not part from it yet, though never was fitter time nor greater cause for it!

ISABELLA: As you desire the praise of a virgin!

LIVIA: Good sorrow! I would do thee any kindess! *(Pause, she seems to suffer.)* Let it suffice, you may refuse this fool, or you may take him as you see occasion. You cannot be enforced.

ISABELLA: Sweet aunt, deal plainer.

LIVIA: Say I should trust you now upon an oath, and give you in a secret that would start you. How am I sure of you, in faith and silence?

ISABELLA: Equal assurance may I find in mercy, as you for that in me.

LIVIA: It shall suffice. Then know, however custom has made good, for reputation's sake, the names of niece and aunt 'twixt you and I, we are nothing less.

ISABELLA: How's that?

LIVIA: I told you I should start your blood. You are no more allied to any of us than the merest stranger is, or one begot at Naples when the husband lies at Rome. Did never the report of that famed Spaniard, Marquess of Coria, since your time was ripe for understanding, fill your ear with wonder?

ISABELLA: Yes, what of him? I have heard his deeds of honour often related when we lived in Naples.

LIVIA: You heard the praises of your father, then.

ISABELLA: My father!

LIVIA: That was he. But all the business so carefully and so discreetly carried that fame received no spot by it, not a blemish. How weak his commands now, whom you call father? How vain all his enforcements, your obedience? And what a largeness in your will and liberty to take or reject, or to do both? For fools will serve to father wise men's children—all this you have time to think on. Oh, my wench, nothing overthrows our sex but indiscretion! But keep your thoughts to yourself, from all the world, kindred or dearest friend—nay, I entreat you, from him that all this while you have called uncle; and though you love him dearly, as I know his deserts claim as much even from a stranger, yet let not him know this, I prithee do not.

ISABELLA: Believe my oath, I will not.

LIVIA: Why, well said . . . *(She turns to go.)* Who shows more craft to undo a maidenhead, I'll resign my part to her. (HIPPOLITO *comes in.*) She's thine own, go. (LIVIA *goes out.*)

ISABELLA: Have I passed so much time in ignorance, and never had the means to know myself till this blest hour! Thanks to her virtuous pity that brought it now to light—would I had known it but one day sooner, he had then received in favours what, poor gentleman, he took in bitter words! *(She turns to him.)* Prithee, forgive me. I did but chide in jest; the best loves use it sometimes, it sets an edge upon affection. When we invite our best friends to a feast, 'tis not all sweetmeats that we set before them, there's somewhat sharp and salt both to whet the appetite and make 'em taste their wine well. So, methinks, after a friendly, sharp and savoury chiding, a kiss tastes wondrous well and full of the grape—*(She kisses him.)* How thinks't thou, does't not?

HIPPOLITO: 'Tis so excellent, I know not how to praise it, what to say to it!

ISABELLA: The marriage shall go forward.

HIPPOLITO: With the ward? Are you in earnest?

ISABELLA: Should my father provide a worse fool yet I'd have him either. The worse the better. So discretion love me, desert and judgement, I have content sufficient. Pray make your love no stranger, sir, that's all. *(She goes out.)*

HIPPOLITO: Never came joys so unexpectedly to meet desires in man. How came she thus? But I'm thankful for it. this marriage now must of necessity go forward, it is the only veil wit can devise to keep our acts hid from sin-piercing eyes.

Scene Five

GUARDIANO *and* LIVIA.

LIVIA: How, sir, a gentlewoman so young, so fair, as you set forth, spied from the widow's window?

GUARDIANO: She!

LIVIA: Our Sunday-dinner woman?

GUARDIANO: And Thursday-supper woman, the same still. I know not how she came by her, but I'll swear she's the prime gallant for a face in Florence, and no doubt other parts follow their leader. The duke himself first spied her at the window, then in a rapture, as if admiration were poor when it were single, beckoned me, and pointed to the wonder warily. I never knew him so infinitely taken with a woman, nor can I blame his appetite, she's a creature able to draw a state from serious business. What course shall we devise? He has spoken twice now.

LIVIA: Twice? I long myself to see this absolute creature that wins the heart of love and praise so much.

GUARDIANO: Shall you entreat her company? I would 'twere done, the duke waits the good hour, and I wait the good fortune that may spring from it. (FABRITIO *comes in.*) Signor Fabritio!

FABRITIO: Oh, sir, I bring an alteration in my mouth now! My daughter loves him.

GUARDIANO: What, does she, sir?

FABRITIO: No talk but of the ward, she would have him to choose 'above all men she ever saw.

GUARDIANO: Why, then sir, if you'll have me speak my thoughts, I smell 'twill be a match.

FABRITIO: Ay, and a sweet young couple if I have any judgement.

GUARDIANO: Let her be sent tomorrow before noon, and handsomely tricked up.

FABRITIO: I warrant you for handsome. I will see her things laid ready, every one in order, and have some part of her tricked up tonight. 'Twas a use her mother had when invited to an early wedding; she'ld dress her head o'ernight, sponge up herself, and give her neck three lathers.

GUARDIANO: Ne'er a halter?

FABRITIO: On with her chain of pearl, her ruby bracelets, lay ready all her tricks and jiggambobs.

GUARDIANO: So must her daughter. (FABRITIO *goes out.*)

LIVIA: How he sweats in the foolish zeal of fatherhood... and here comes his sweet son-in-law that shall be. They're both allied in wit before the marriage, what will they be hereafter, when they are nearer? *(She goes out.)*

THE WARD *and* SORDIDO *enter, with shuttlecocks and battledores.*

GUARDIANO: Now, young heir!

WARD: What's the next business after shuttlecock?

GUARDIANO: Tomorrow you shall see the gentlewoman must be your wife.

WARD: There's even another thing too must be kept up with a pair of battledores. My wife! What can she do?

GUARDIANO: Nay, that's a question you should ask yourself, ward, when you're alone together.

WARD: That's as I list! A wife's to be asked anywhere, I hope. I'll ask her in a congregation, if I have a mind to it, and so save a licence.

SORDIDO: Let me be at the choosing of your beloved, if you
    desire a woman of good parts.
WARD: Thou shalt, sweet Sordido!
SORDIDO: I have a plaguey guess. Let me alone to see what
    she is. If I but look upon her—'way, I know all the faults to a
    hair you may refuse her for.
WARD: Dost thou? I prithee let me hear 'em, Sordido.
SORDIDO: Well, mark 'em then. I have 'em all in rhyme.

> The wife your gardener ought to tenderr
> Should be pretty, straight and slender;
> Her hair not short, her foot not long,.
> Her hand not huge, not too loud her tongue;
> No pearl in eye nor ruby in her nose,
> No burn or cut but what the catalogue shows.
> She must have teeth, and that no black ones,
> And kiss most sweet when she does smack once;
> Her skin must be both white and plumpt,
> Her body straight, not hopper rumped,
> Or wriggle sideways like a crab.
> She must be neither slut nor drab,
> Nor go too splay-foot with her shoes
> To make her smock lick up the dews.
> And two things more which I forgot to tell ye;
> She neither must have bump in back nor belly.

These are the faults which will not make her pass.
WARD: And if I spy not these am I a rank ass!
SORDIDO: You should see her naked, for that's the ancient
    order.
WARD: See her naked? That were good sport, in faith, but
    stay! How if she should desire to see me so too? I were in a
    sweet case, then; such a foul skin!
SORDIDO: But you have a clean shirt, sir, and that makes
    amends.
WARD: 'Faith, choosing of a wench in a huge farthingale is
    like buying of ware under a great penthouse; what with the
    deceit of one, and the false light of the other, mark my
    speeches, he may have a diseased wench in his bed, and
    rotten stuff in his breeches! (*They whoop with laughter, go
    out.*)
LIVIA (*entering with* THE MOTHER). Widow, come, come!
    I have a great quarrel to you, 'faith, I must chide you, that you

must be sent for! You cannot be more welcome to any house in Florence.

MOTHER: My thanks must needs acknowledge so much, madam.

LIVIA: I sit here sometimes whole days without company! I know you are alone, too, why should we not we, like two kind neighbours, then, supply the wants of one another, having tongue-discourse, experience in the world, and such kind helps to laugh down time, and meet age merrily?

MOTHER: Age, madam! You speak mirth. 'Tis at my door, but long journey from your ladyship yet.

LIVIA: My faith, I'm nine and thirty, every stroke, wench, and 'tis a general observation, wives or widows, we account ourselves then old, when young men's eyes leave looking at us. Come, now, I have thy company I'll not part with it till after supper.

MOTHER: Yes, I must crave pardon, madam—

LIVIA: I swear you shall stay supper.

MOTHER: Some other time I will make bold—

GUARDIANO: No, pray stay, widow.

LIVIA: Faith, she shall not go. Do you think I'll be forsworn? (*She brings table and chess*)

MOTHER: 'Tis a great while till supper time. I'll take my leave then now, madam, and come again in the evening—

LIVIA: In the evening! By my troth, wench, you have great business, sure, to sit alone at home! I wonder strangely what pleasure you take in it! Come, we'll to chess or draughts; there are an hundred tricks to drive out time till supper, never fear.

MOTHER: I'll make but one step home and return straight, madam.

LIVIA: I'll not trust you, you use more excuses to your kind friends than ever I knew any! What business can you have, if you be sure you have locked the door?

MOTHER: As good as tell her now, then, for she will know. I have always found her a most friendly lady. (*She turns to* LIVIA.) To tell you truth. I left a gentlewoman sitting all alone, which is uncomfortable, especially to young bloods.

LIVIA: What gentlewoman? Pish! Another excuse!

MOTHER: Wife to my son indeed, but not known, madam, to any but yourself.

LIVIA: Now I beshrew you! Could you be so unkind to her and me, to come and not bring her?

MOTHER: I feared to be too bold. And she's a stranger,

madam.

LIVIA: The more should be her welcome. Make some amends, and fetch her, go.

MOTHER *(rising to go)*. It must be carried wondrous privately from my son's knowledge; he'll break out in storms else. (*She goes out.*)

LIVIA: Now comes in the heat of your part.

GUARDIANO: True, I know it, lady, and if I be out, may the duke banish me from all employments, wanton or serious. (BIANCA *comes in, curtsies.*)

LIVIA: Gentlewoman, you are most welcome, trust me, you are, as courtesy can make one, or respect due to the presence of you.

BIANCA: I give you thanks, lady.

LIVIA: I heard you were alone, and it had appeared an ill condition in me to have kept your company from you and left you all solitary. *(To* MOTHER.) Come widow—look you, lady, here's our business. Are we not well employed, think you? An old quarrel between us, that will never be at an end. I pray, sit down forsooth, if you have the patience to look upon two weak and tedious gamesters...

GUARDIANO: 'Faith, madam, set these by till evening. The gentlewoman, being a stranger, would take more delight to see your rooms and pictures.

LIVIA: Marry, good sir, and well remembered! I beseech you show 'em her, that will beguile time well. Here, take these keys, show her the monument too—and that's a thing everyone sees not, you can witness that, widow!

MOTHER: And that's a worth sight indeed, madam.

BIANCA: Kind lady, I fear I came to be a trouble to you, and to this courteous gentleman that wears a kindess in his breast so noble and bounteous.

GUARDIANO: If you but give acceptance to my service, you do the greatest grace and honour to me that courtesy can merit.

BIANCA: I pray you lead, sir.

LIVIA: After a game or two, we are for you, gentlefolks... *(They go out.* LIVIA *plays chess.)* Alas, poor widow, I shall be too hard for thee.

MOTHER: You're cunning at the game, I'll be sworn, madam...

LIVIA: It will be found so, ere I give you over... She that can place her man well...

MOTHER: As you do, madam...

LIVIA: As I shall, wench, can never lose her game. Nay, nay, the black king's mine.

MOTHER: Cry you mercy, madam.

LIVIA: And this my queen.

MOTHER: I see it now.

LIVIA: Here's a duke will strike a sure stroke for the game anon; your pawn cannot come back to relieve itself.

MOTHER: I know that, madam.

LIVIA: You play well the whilst. How she belies her skill. I give you check and mate to your white king, simplicity itself.

MOTHER: Well, ere now, lady, I have seen the fall of subtlety. Jest on! What remedy but patience! (GUARDIANO *and* BIANCA, *above*)

BIANCA: Trust me, sir, mine eye never met with fairer ornaments.

GUARDIANO: Nay, livelier, I'm persuaded, neither Florence nor Venice can produce.

BIANCA: Sir, my opinion takes your part highly.

GUARDIANO: There's a better piece yet, than all these... (*Enter unseen the* DUKE.)

BIANCA: Not possible, sir!

GUARDIANO: Believe it. You'll say so when you see it. Turn but your eye now. *(He goes out.)*

BIANCA: Oh, sir!

DUKE: He's gone, beauty! Pish, not look after him, he's but a vapour that when the sun appears is seen no more.

BIANCA: Oh, treachery to honour!

DUKE: Prithee, tremble not. I feel thy breast shake like a turtle panting under a loving hand that makes much on't. Why art so fearful? As I'm friend to brightness, there's nothing but respect and honour near thee. You know me, you have seen me; here's a heart can witness I've seen thee.

BIANCA: The more's my danger.

DUKE: The more's my happiness. Pish, strive not, sweet! This strength were excellent employed in love, now, but here 'tis spent amiss. Strive not to seek thy liberty and keep me still in prison.

BIANCA: Oh, my lord!

DUKE: Take warning, I beseech thee. Thou seem'st to me a creature so composed of gentleness I should be sorry the least force should lay an unkind touch upon thee.

BIANCA: Oh, my extremity! My lord, what seek you?

DUKE: Love.

BIANCA: 'Tis gone already, I have a husband.

DUKE: That's a single comfort. Take a friend to him.

BIANCA: That's a double mischief, or else there's no religion.

DUKE: Do not tremble at fears of thine own making.

BIANCA: Nor great lord, make me not bold with death and deeds of ruin because they fear not you.

DUKE: Sure, I think thou know'st the way to please me. I affect a passionate pleading above an easy yielding—but never pitied any. They deserve none that will not pity me. I can command. Think upon that.

BIANCA: Why should you seek, sir, to take away that you can never give?

DUKE: But I give better in exchange! Wealth, honour! She that is fortunate in a duke's favour lights on a tree that bears all women's wishes. If your own mother saw you pluck fruit there, she would commend your wit and praise the time of your nativity. Take hold of glory. Do not I know you have cast away your life upon necessities, means merely doubtful to keep you in indifferent health and fashion—a thing I heard too lately and soon pitied...? And can you be so much your beauty's enemy to kiss away a month or two in wedlock, and weep whole years in wants for ever after? Come, play the wise wench and provide for ever... *(They go out.)*

LIVIA: Did I not say my duke would fetch you over, widow?

MOTHER: I think you spoke in earnest when you said it, madam...

LIVIA: And my black king makes all the haste he can, too, I have given thee blind mate twice...!

MOTHER: You may see, madam, my eyes begin to fail...

LIVIA: I'll swear they do...

GUARDIANO *(entering)*. I can but smile as often as I think on it! How prettily the poor fool was beguiled, how unexpectedly! It is a witty age, never were finer snares for women's honesties than are devised in these days. Yet to prepare her stomach by degrees to Cupid's feast, I showed her naked pictures by the way—a bit to stay the appetite...

LIVIA: The game's even at the best now. You may see widow, how all things draw to an end. Has not my duke bestirred himself?

MOTHER: Yes, 'faith, madam, he has done all the mischief in this game...

BIANCA *(entering)*. Now bless me from a blasting! I saw that

now fearful for any woman's eye to look on. Infectious mists
and mildews hang at his eyes, the weather of a doomsday
dwells upon him. Yet, since mine honour's leprous, why
should I preserve that fair that caused the leprosy? Come
poison all at once! Thou in whose baseness the bane of virtue
broods, I'm bound in soul eternally to curse thy smooth-
browed treachery that wore the fair veil of a friendly
welcome! And I a stranger, think upon it! Murders piled up
upon a guilty spirit at his last breath will not lie heavier than
this betraying act upon thy conscience. I'm made bold now,
I thank thy treachery. Sin and I'm acquainted, no couple
greater.

GUARDIANO: Well, so the duke loves me I fare not much
  amiss, then. Two great feasts do seldom come together in
  one day.

BIANCA: What, still at it, mother?

MOTHER: You see we sit by it. Are you so soon returned?
  You have not seen all, since, surely?

BIANCA: That have I, Mother, the monument and all! 'Faith,
  I have seen that I little thought to see in the morning when I
  rose...

MOTHER: Nay, so I told you before you saw it, it would prove
  worth your sight. I give you great thanks for my daughter,
  sir, and all your kindness towards her.

GUARDIANO: Oh, good widow! Much good may it do
  her—forty weeks hence, in faith...!

LIVIA *(rising)*. We'll walk to supper. (*To* BIANCA.) Will it
  please you, gentlewoman?

BIANCA: Thanks, virtuous lady—you are a damned bawd!
  I'll follow you, forsooth. Pray take my mother in, this
  gentleman and I vow not to part... (*She and* GUARDIANO
  go out. MOTHER *leads the way.)*

LIVIA: Are you so bitter? 'Tis but want of use, her tender
  modesty is sea-sick a little, being not accustomed to the
  breaking billow of woman's wavering faith, blown with
  temptations. Sin tastes at the first draught like wormwood
  bitter, but drunk again, 'tis nectar even after.

Scene Six

THE MOTHER.

MOTHER: I would my son would either keep at home or I were in my grave! She was not but one day abroad but ever since she's grown so cutted, there's no speaking to her. Whether the sight of great cheer at my lady's, and such mean fare at home, work discontent in her, I know not, but I'm sure she's strangely altered. I'll never keep daughter-in-law in the house with me again if I had a hundred.

BIANCA *(entering)*. This is the strangest house for all defects as ever gentlewoman made shift withal to pass away her love in! Why is there not a cushion cloth of drawn work, or some fair cut-work pinned up in my bed-chamber, a silver and gilt casting bottle hung by it?

MOTHER: She talks of great things here my whole state's not worth...

BIANCA: Never a green silk quilt is there in the house, mother, to cast upon my bed?

MOTHER: No, by troth is there! Nor orange-tawny, neither.

BIANCA: Here's a house for a young gentlewoman to be got with child in!

MOTHER: What, cannot children be begot, think you, without gilt casting-bottles? 'Tis an old saying, 'one may keep good cheer in a mean house'.

BIANCA: Troth, you speak wondrous well for your old house here, 'twill shortly fall down at your feet to thank you. Must I live in want because my fortune matched me with your son? I ask less now than what I had at home when I was a maid, kept short of that which a wife knows she must have, nay, and will! Will, mother, if she be not a fool born. And report went of me that I could wrangle for what I wanted when I was two hours old...! *(She goes out.)*

MOTHER: When she first lighted here, I told her then how mean she should find things—she was pleased forsooth! None better! I laid open all defects to her, she was contented still! But the devil's in her. What course shall I think on? She frets me so...

LEANTIO *(entering)*. How near I am now to happiness that earth exceeds not. Not another like it! I scent the air of blessings when I come but near the house! Honest wedlock is

like a banqueting house built in a garden, when base lust
with all her powders, paintings and best pride is but a fair
house built by a ditch side. Now for a welcome able to draw
men's envies upon man! After a five days' fast she'll be so
greedy now, and cling about me, I take care how I shall be rid
of her! And here it begins!

BIANCA *and* MOTHER *enter.*

BIANCA: Oh, sir, you are welcome home.

LEANTIO: Is that all? Why this? Sure you are not well,
Bianca. How dost, prithee?

BIANCA: I have been better than I am.

LEANTIO: Alas, I thought so.

BIANCA: Nay, I have been worse, too, that now you see me,
sir.

LEANTIO: I'm glad thou mend'st yet. I feel my heart mend,
too. How came it to thee? Has anything disliked thee in my
absence?

BIANCA: No, certain... I have had the best content that
Florence can afford...

LEANTIO: Thou mak'st the best of it. Speak, mother, what's
the cause? You must needs know.

MOTHER: Troth, I know none, son. Let her speak herself.

BIANCA: Methinks this house stands nothing to my mind,
I'ld have some pleasant lodging in the high street, sir. Or if it
were near the court, that were much better—'tis a sweet
recreation for a gentlewoman to stand in a bay window and
see gallants.

LEANTIO: Now, I have another temper, a mere stranger to
that of yours, it seems. I should delight to see none but
yourself.

BIANCA: I praise not that. Too fond is as unseemly as too
churlish. I would not have a husband of that proneness to
kiss me before company, for a world! Beside, 'tis tedious to
see one thing still, sir, be it the best that ever heart affected.
You are learned sir, and, know I speak not ill. 'Tis full as
virtuous for a woman's eye to look on several men as for her
heart, sir, to be fixed on one...

LEANTIO: Now thou com'st home to me! A kiss for that
word!

BIANCA: No matter for a kiss, sir, let is pass. Let's talk of
other business and forget it. What news now of the pirates?
Any stirring?

MOTHER: I'm glad he's here yet to see her tricks himself. I had lied monstrously if I had told 'em first.

LEANTIO: Speak, what's the humour, sweet, you make your lip so strange? This is not wont.

BIANCA: Is there no kindness betwixt man and wife unless they make a pigeon-house of friendship and be still billing? Alas, sir, think of the world, how we shall live, grow serious. We have been married a whole fortnight now.

LEANTIO: How, a whole fortnight! Is that long? *(A knock.)* Who's there, now? Withdraw you, Bianca, thou art a gem no stranger's eye must see, however thou please now to look dull on me. *(She goes out. A MESSENGER enters.)* You're welcome, sir. To whom your business, pray?

MESSENGER: To one I see not here, now.

LEANTIO: Who should that be?

MESSENGER: A young gentlewoman I was sent to.

LEANTIO: A young gentlewoman?

MESSENGER: Ay, sir, about sixteen. Why look you so wildly?

LEANTIO: At your strange error. You have mistook the house, there's none such here, I assure you.

MESSENGER: I assure you, too. The man sent me cannot be mistook.

LEANTIO: Why, who is it sent you, sir?

MESSENGER: The duke.

LEANTIO: The duke! Troth, shall I tell you, sir, it is the most erroneous business that e'er your honest pains were abused with. His grace has been most wondrous ill-informed. Pray so return it, sir. What should her name be?

MESSENGER: Then I shall tell you straight, too. Bianca Capello.

LEANTIO: How, sir, Bianca? What do you call the other?

MESSENGER: Capello. Sir, it seems you know no such, then?

LEANTIO: I never heard of the name.

MESSENGER: Then 'tis a sure mistake. I will return and seek no further. *(He goes.)*

LEANTIO: Come forth, Bianca. Thou art betrayed, I fear me.

BIANCA *(appearing)*. Betrayed? How, sir?

LEANTIO: The duke knows thee.

BIANCA: How should the duke know me? Can you guess, mother?

MOTHER: Not I with all my wits. Sure, we kept house close.

LEANTIO: Kept close! Not all the locks in Italy can keep you women so! You have been gadding, and ventured out a twilight to the court-green yonder, without your masks. I'll be hanged else! Thou hast been seen, Bianca, by some stranger. Never excuse it.

BIANCA: I'll not seek the way, sir. Do you think you have married me to mew me up not to be seen? What would you make of me?

LEANTIO: A good wife, nothing else.

BIANCA: Why, so are some that are seen every day, else the devil take 'em.

LEANTIO: No more, then. I believe all virtuous in thee without an argument. 'Twas but thy hard chance to be seen somewhere...

MOTHER: Now I can tell you son, the time and place!

LEANTIO: When? Where?

MOTHER: What wits have I! When you last took your leave, if you remember, you left us both at window. And not the third part of an hour after the duke passed by in great solemnity. He looked up twice to the window.

LEANTIO: Looked he up twice! And could you take no warning?

MOTHER: Why, once may do as much harm, so, as a thousand, do you not know one spark has fired an house as well as a a whole furnace?

LEANTIO: My heart flames for it! Yet let's be wise and keep all smothered closely. I have bethought a means. Is the door fast?

MOTHER: I locked it myself after him.

LEANTIO: You know, mother, at the end of the dark parlour there's a place so artificially contrived no search could ever find it. There will I lock my life's best treasure up. Bianca!

BIANCA: Would you keep me closer yet? Have you the conscience?

LEANTIO: Why, are you so insensible of your danger to ask that now? The duke himself has sent for you!

BIANCA: Has he so! And you the man would never yet vouchsafe to tell me of it till now. You show your loyalty and honesty at once, and so, farewell, sir.

LEANTIO: Bianca, whither now?

BIANCA: Why, to the duke, sir, you say he sent for me.

LEANTIO: But thou dost not mean to go, I hope?

BIANCA: No? I shall prove unmannerly, rude and uncivil, mad, and imitate you? Come, mother, come, follow his humour no longer. We shall all be executed for treason shortly.

MOTHER: Not I, in faith. I'll first obey the duke, and taste of a good banquet. I'm of thy mind.

BIANCA: Why, here's an old wench would trot into bawd now for a piece of fruit or marzipan! (*They go out.*)

LEANTIO: Oh, thou the ripe of time of man's misery, wedlock, when all his thoughts, like over-laden trees, crack with the fruits they bear, in cares and jealousies. What a peace he has he that never marries! If he knew the benefit he enjoyed, or had the fortune to come and speak with me, he should know then the infinite wealth he had, and discern rightly the greatness of his treature by my loss. Nay, what a quietness he has above mine, that wears his youth out in a strumpet's arms and never spends more care upon a woman than at the time of lust, but walks away, and if he finds her dead at his return, his pity is soon done. But all the fears, shames, jealousies, costs and troubles, and still renewed cares of a marriage bed live in the issue when the wife is dead . . .

MESSENGER (*entering*). Though you were pleased just now to pin an error on me, you must not shift another in your stead too. The duke has sent for you.

LEANTIO: How, for me? I see then, 'tis my theft. Well, I'm not the first has stolen away a maid! (*They hurry out.*)

Scene Seven

A banquet.

GUARDIANO: Take you especial note of such a gentle-woman, she's here on purpose. I have invited her, her father and her uncle to this banquet.

WARD: 'Faith, I should know her now, among a thousand women. A little pretty, deft and tidy thing, you say?

GUARDIANO: Right.

WARD: With a lusty, sprouting sprig in her hair?

GUARDIANO: Thou goest the right way still. Take one mark more. Thou shalt never find her hand out of her uncle's. The love of kindred never yet stuck closer than theirs to one another. He that weds her marries her uncle's heart, too.

WARD: Say you so, sir! Then I'll be asked in the church to both of 'em!

GUARDIANO: Fall back, here comes the duke!

WARD: He brings a gentlewoman, I should fall forward, rather!

DUKE: Come Bianca, of purpose sent into the world to show perfection once in woman. I'll believe henceforward they have every one a soul, too, against all the uncourteous opinions that man's uncivil rudeness ever held of 'em. Glory of Florence, light into mine arms.

LEANTIO *enters.*

BIANCA: Yon comes a grudging man will chide you, sir. The storm is now in his heart, and would get nearer and fall here if it durst—it pours down yonder.

DUKE: If that be he, the weather shall soon clear. Listen, and I'll tell thee how. (*Whispers to her.*)

LEANTIO: A kissing, too? I see 'tis plain lust now, adultery boldened. What will it prove anon, when 'tis stuffed full of wine and sweetmeats, being so impudent fasting?

DUKE: We have heard of your good parts, sir, which we honour with our embrace and love. Is not the captainship of Rouens' citadel, since the late deceased, supplied by any yet?

GUARDIANO: By none, my lord.

DUKE: Take it, the place is yours, then. (LEANTIO *kneels.*) And as faithfulness and desert grows, our favour shall grow with it. Rise now, the captain of our fort at Rouens!

LEANTIO: The service of whole life give your grace thanks. (*Aside.*) This is some good yet, and more than ever I looked for—a fine bit to stay a cukold's stomach! All preferment that springs from sin and lust, it shoots up quickly, as gardeners' crops do in the rottenest grounds.

LIVIA: Is that your son, widow?

MOTHER: Yes, did your ladyship never know that till now?

LIVIA: No, trust me, did I. Nor ever truly felt the power of love and pity to a man, till now I knew him. I have enough to buy me my desires, and yet to spare, that's one good comfort. Hark you? Pray let me speak with you, sir, before you go...

DUKE: Here's a health now, gallants, to the best beauty at this day in Florence!

BIANCA: Whoe'r she be, she shall not go unpledged, sir...

DUKE: Here's to thy health, Bianca...

BIANCA: Nothing comes more welcome to that name than your grace...

LEANTIO: So, so! Here stands the poor thief now that stole the treasure, and he's not thought on.

DUKE: Methinks there is no spirit amongst us, gallants, but what divinely sparkles from the eyes of bright Bianca—we sat all in darkness but for that splendour. Who was it told us lately of a match-making rite, a marriage-tender?

GUARDIANO: 'Twas I, my lord.

DUKE: 'Twas you indeed. Where is she?

GUARDIANO: This is the gentlewoman.

FABRITIO: My lord, my daughter.

WARD: The ape's so little, I shall scarce feel her. I have seen almost as tall as she sold in the fair for tenpence...

FABRITIO: She has the full qualities of a gentlewoman, I have brought her up to music, dancing and whatnot, that may commend her sex and stir her husband...

WARD: See how she simpers—as if marmalade would not melt in her mouth...

DUKE: And which is he?

GUARDIANO: This young heir, my lord.

DUKE: What is he brought up to?

WARD: To cat and trap.

GUARDIANO: My lord, he's a great ward, wealthy but simple. His parts consist in acres.

DUKE: Oh, wise acres!

GUARDIANO: Y'have spoke him in a word, sir!

BIANCA: 'Las, poor gentlewoman, she's ill bestead, unless she's dealt the wiselier and laid in more provision for her youth. Fools will not keep in summer.

LEANTIO: No, nor such wives from whores in winter.

DUKE (*to* FABRITIO). Yea, the voice too, sir?

FABRITIO: Ay, and a sweet breast too, my lord, I hope, or I have cast away my money wisely—she took her pricksong earlier, my lord, that any of her kindred ever did.

DUKE: Let's turn to a better banquet, then. For music bids the soul of man to feast! (*Music.*)

LEANTIO: True, and damnation has taught you that wisdom. You can take gifts, too! Oh, that music mocks me!

LIVIA: I am as dumb to any language now but love's, as one that never learned to speak! I am not yet so old, but he may think of me. My own fault—I have been idle a long time.

ISABELLA (*singing*): What harder chance can fall to woman,
Who was born to cleave to some man,
Than to bestow her time, youth, beauty,
Life's observance, honour, duty,
On a thing for no use good
But to make physic work, or blood
Force fresh in an old lady's cheek?
So that would be
Mother of fools, let her compound with me...

WARD: Here's a tune indeed! Pish! I would rather hear one
ballad sung in the nose now, of the lamentable drowning of
fat sheep and oxen, than all these simpering tunes played
upon cat-guts and sung by little kitlings.

FABRITIO (*to* GUARDIANO). Will it please you now, sir, to
entreat your ward to take her by the hand and lead her in a
dance before the duke?

WARD: Dance with her! Not I, sweet guardiner, do not urge
my heart to it, 'tis clean against my blood. Dance with a
stranger!

GUARDIANO: Why, who shall take her, then?

WARD: Look, there's her uncle! Perhaps he knows the
manner of her dancing, too?

GUARDIANO: Thou'lt be an ass, still.

WARD: Ay. All that 'uncle' shall not fool me out...

GUARDIANO (*to* HIPPOLITO). I must entreat you, sir, to
take your niece and dance with her. My ward's a little wilful,
he would have you show him the way.

HIPPOLITO:Me, sir! He shall command it at all hours, pray
tell him so.

GUARDIANO: I thank you for him. He has not wit himself,
sir.

The Dance. Enter, surreptitiously, SORDIDO.

GUARDIANO (*to* WARD). Do it when I bid you, sir...

WARD: I'll venture but a hornpipe with her, guardiner, or
some such married man's dance...

WARD: Well, venture something sir! (*Turns.* SORDIDO
comes to THE WARD's *side.*)

WARD: Here she's come again. Mark her now, Sordido...
(*He declares half publicly.*)
Plain men dance the measures, the cinquepence the gay;
Cuckolds dance the hornpipe, and farmers dance the hay;

Your soldiers dance the round, and maidens that grow big,
Your drunkards the canaries, your whore and bawd, the jig.
Here's your eight kind of dancers—he that find the ninth,
Let him pay the minstrels. (*He goes to dance.*)

DUKE: Oh, here he appears once in his own person! I thought
he would have married her by attorney, and lain with her so,
too. (THE WARD *ridiculously imitates* HIPPOLITO.)

BIANCA: Methinks, if he would take some voyage when he's
married, dangerous or long enough, and scarce be seen once
in nine year together, a wife them might make indifferent
shift to be content with him...

THE WARD *and* ISABELLA *dance.*

ISABELLA: And how do you like me, now, sir?

WARD: 'Faith, so well I never mean to part with thee,
sweetheart, under some sixteen children.

GUARDIANO: How now, ward and nephew, speak, is it so,
or not?

WARD: 'Tis so, we are both agreed, sir. (GUARDIANO *bows
to* THE DUKE.)

DUKE: My thanks to all your loves! Come, fair Bianca, we
have took special care of you, and provided your lodging near
us now.

BIANCA: Once more, our thanks to all.

ALL: All blest honours guard you!

LEANTIO: Oh, hast thou left me then, Bianca, utterly!
Bianca, now I miss thee—oh, return, and save the faith of
woman. I never felt the loss of thee till now, 'tis an affliction
of greater weight than youth was made to bear!

LIVIA: Sweet sir!

LEANTIO: As long as mine eye saw thee, I half enjoyed
thee...

LIVIA: Sir?

LEANTIO: Canst thou forget the dear pains my love took,
how it has watched whole nights together in all weathers for
thee, yet stood in heart more merry than the tempests that
sung about mine ears, and then received thee from thy
father's window into these arms at midnight, when we
embraced as if we had been statues only made for it, to show
art's life, so silent were our comforts...

LIVIA: This makes me madder to enjoy him now. Sir!

LEANTIO: Cry mercy, lady! What would you say to me? My
sorrow makes me so unmannerly, I had quite forgot you.

LIVIA: Nothing, but even in pity to that passion, would give your grief good counsel.

LEANTIO: Marry, and welcome, lady, it never could come better.

LIVIA: You missed your fortunes when you met with her, sir. Young gentlemen that only love for beauty, they love not wisely; such a marriage rather proves the destruction of affection. It brings on want, and want's the key of whoredom. I think you had small means with her?

LEANTIO: Oh, not any, lady.

LIVIA: Alas, poor gentleman! What mean'st thou, sir, quite to undo thyself with thine own kind heart? Thou art too good and pitiful to woman. Thank thy lucky stars for this blest fortune that rids the summer of thy youth so well from many beggars that had lain a-sunning in thy beams only else till thou hadst wasted the whole days of thy life in heat and labour. What would you say now to a creature found as pitiful to you as it were even sent on purpose from the whole sex general to requite all that kindness you have shown to it?

LEANTIO: What's that, madam?

LIVIA: Could'st thou love such a one that, blow all fortunes, would never see thee want? Nay, more, maintain thee to thine enemy's envy? And shalt not spend a care for it, stir a thought, nor break a sleep—unless love's music waked thee, no storm of fortune should. Look upon me, and know that woman.

LEANTIO: Oh, my life's wealth, Bianca!

LIVIA: He's vexed in mind. I came too soon to him. Where's my discretion now, my skill, my judgement? I'm cunning in all arts but my own love. (*She goes out.*)

LEANTIO: Is she my wife till death, yet no more mine? Methinks by right I should not now be living, and then 'twere all well! She's gone forever—utterly! There is as much redemption as a soul from hell as a fair woman's body from his palace! Why should my love last longer than her truth? What is there good in woman to be loved when only that which makes her so has left her? My safest course, for health of mind and body is to turn my heart and hate her, most extremely hate!

LIVIA (*returning*): I have tried all ways I can, and have not power to keep from sight of him. How are you now, sir?

LEANTIO: I feel a better ease, madam...

LIVIA: You never saw the beauty of my house yet, nor how

abundantly fortune has blessed me. I have enough, sir, to make my friend a rich man in my life, a great man at my death. If you want anything and spare to speak, troth, I'll condemn you for a wilful man, sir.

LEANTIO: Why sure, this can be but the flattery of some dream...

LIVIA: Now, by this kiss, my love, my soul, my riches, 'tis all true substance. Take what you list, the gallanter you go, the more you please me, but to me only sir, wear your heart of constant stuff. Do but you love enough, I'll give enough.

Scene Eight

The Palace. CARDINAL, DUKE *and* BIANCA.

CARDINAL: You vowed never to keep a strumpet more, and are you now so swift in your desires to knit your honours and your life fast to her? Must marriage, that immaculate robe of honour, be now made the garment of leprosy and foulness? Is this penitence, to sanctify hot lust?

DUKE: The path now I tread, is honest. I vowed no more to keep a sensual woman—'tis done. I mean to make a lawful wife of her.

CARDINAL: Do not grow too cunning for your soul, good brother! Is it enough to use adulterous thefts, and then take sanctuary in marriage?

BIANCA: Sir, I have read you over all this while in silence, and I find great knowledge in you, and severe learning; yet 'mongst all your virtues I see not charity written, which some call the first born of religion, and I wonder I cannot see it...

DUKE: I kiss thee for that spirit! Thou hast praised thy wit a modest way! (*He turns back to* CARDINAL.) Here y'are bitter without cause, brother. What I vow, I keep safe as you your conscience. All this needs not. I taste more wrath in it than I do religion, and envy more than goodness... (CARDINAL *goes out.*)

BIANCA: How strangely woman's fortune comes about! This was the farthest way to come to me that knew me born in Venice and there with many jealous eyes brought up. 'Tis not good, in sadness, to keep a maid so strict in her young days. Restraint breeds wandering thoughts. I'll never use any girl of mine so strictly—however they're kept, their fortunes find 'em out.

LEANTIO (*entering beneath her window*). I long to see how my despiser looks now she's come here to court, these are her lodgings! I took her out of no such window, I remember, first. That was a great deal lower, and less carved ...

BIANCA: How now, what silkworm's this, in the name of pride! What, is it he? Methinks you are wondrous brave, sir!

LEANTIO: A sumptuous lodging!

BIANCA: You have an excellent suit, there.

LEANTIO: A chair of velvet!

BIANCA: Is your coat lined through, sir? Who's your shoemaker? He has made you a neat boot.

LEANTIO: Will you have a pair? The duke will lend you spurs.

BIANCA: Yes, when I ride.

LEANTIO: 'Tis a brave life you lead.

BIANCA: I could never see you in such good clothes in my time.

LEANTIO: In your time?

BIANCA: Sure, I think, sir, we both thrive best asunder.

LEANTIO: Y'are a whore.

BIANCA: Oh, sir, you give me thanks for your captainship. I thought you had forgot all your good manners.

LEANTIO: And to spite thee as much, look there, there read! Vex! Gnaw! Thou shalt find there I am not pitiless but there was ever still more charity found out than at one proud fool's door.

BIANCA: Y'are simply happy, sir, yet I'll not envy you.

LEANTIO: No, court-saint, not thou! You keep some friend of a new fashion. There's no harm in your devil, he's a suckling, but he will breed teeth shortly, will he not?

BIANCA: Take heed you play not then too long with him.

LEANTIO: Why, here's sin made and never a conscience put it it! Why do I talk to thee of sense or virtue that art as dark as death? To an ignorance darker than thy womb I leave thy perjured soul. A plague will come!

PART TWO

Scene One

LEANTIO, *undressed.*

LEANTIO: We fuck the day to death. And suffocate the night
with tossing. Time stands still, she says so. Rolls back, even.
As for the bed, it's our whole territory, the footboard and the
headboard are the horizons of our estate, rank with the flood
of flesh. Oh, beautiful odour of the utter fuck! And come?
No, never come, for that's to end it. Clerks come, and
butchers prior to a good night's kipping, farmers with their
eight strokes, who's not heard their mechanistic butting? I
know, was I not a clerk myself, and salesman? Oh, the bars
and barmaids of the provinces, dead minds spewing the dead
opinion, dead eyes on the dying bra strap slipping **fuck all
that watery desire** no woman under forty is worth entering!
(LIVIA *enters.*) Did I hurt you? For one moment I thought I
have killed her. We do strive in one another, all bruises and
dragged hair . . .

LIVIA: You hurt me, and I welcome the hurt. I thought once, I
am dying, and I did not mind. I have no indignation left,
surprise, or petty reservation. No thing I won't yield up, nor
thought ashamed· to utter. May I tell you, I have never
wanted to be free of you. All other men I thought, enough,
roll off and leave my premises. The ecstasy of being left,
silence and the reclamation of myself. Not you, though. It's
five days since we stepped outside. Are there still streets, and
what colour are the buses? (*She looks out the window.*) Oh,
people look the same! Two legs and heads down, the shuffle
and the stagger, **repetition of the mundane life!** (*She selects
among the crowd.*) She'll lend a little of her hip, he'll tamper
with a giggle, that one might yield her place to satisfy
persistence, and him mutter as he shudders but **transformation . . .!** (*She turns back to* LEANTIO.) **Yes I am arrogant.**
Do you complain about my arrogance? You made me so,

and I might have died unknowing...

LEANTIO (*at the window*). There has been change here! Look, they paint the lamp posts for the royal wedding!

LIVIA: All this bunting clinging to a dirty world! And look, Bianca in silver paint staring in our bedroom! I heard no workmen hammering!

LEANTIO: The bitch reviles me! Close the shutter!

LIVIA: Even in paint, her ambitious lip...

LEANTIO: And they applaud her, call her innocence!

LIVIA: You never touched her womb, Leantio. Had you done so she could not revile you without wanting you as well. Revile and clamour, clamour and revile. Tell me you don't feel her still, she could give you nothing but shallow prodding, you could not thrust against her heart like you do mine, I promise you.

LEANTIO (*going to her*). I am slave and master to you alone. Above you I struggle with a girl, beneath I submit to the hag who lurks inside your creases, who has not possessed you! Tell me your fuck history, you used and used again whore—

LIVIA: He abuses me...

LEANTIO: Yes! And by abuse I praise you, lavish bitch, hunted and devoured female—

LIVIA: Are we insane? I think it possible we are insane!

LEANTIO: Yes, and good riddance to their sense, their swop of stale banalities!

LIVIA: I would not be a girl again—

LEANTIO: So every woman of your ripeness should say, who finds her match at last! (*He kneels to her.*) Recite to me, who lay in you before me, scratch your memory! (*He kisses her belly.*) I suffer on you, you are my cross, the pain, you know the pain do you, you are a rack also to stretch me on...

LIVIA: Yes, all you know, I do too...

LEANTIO (*stops*). But I do hate Bianca. I wish I could be happy to despise, but no, I hate...

LIVIA: Good! Hate!

LEANTIO: Must I?

LIVIA: Those whose love runs deep dispense no charity. You are no bridegroom whose handshake is free to all, and I no bride all teeth. Through pain of longing we have trod down sickening conviviality. Shudder, shudder at behaviour I tinkled over once. I tinkled then, I did not laugh, and now I find, laughter! Real laughter! Don't suffer shame for proper hates...

LEANTIO: Your brother wants me dead.

LIVIA: My brother! Whose tender honour bruises so! Oh, my honour, my sister is a bint for fucking with the factor! The man's a snob, and coarse for all his culture! Listen—(*She draws him to her.*) The world hates passion. Fornication's all its taste, what's good for telling over dinner, how the empty girl was taken, and she smiles, she smiles in willing collaboration, the used smiling at her usage! (*She releases him, turning away.*) And I tried to tell him! **Absurd undertaking!** (*She laughs.*) Such was his contempt I feared he'd chain me as a lunatic! They think of love as discharge, something in the groin to be delivered, I know them, I do know, did I not giggle over their thin and sour longings? **Hunger!** What do they know of that? Touch me and I know I live! (*He caresses her.*) Beloved man, if you perished tonight in some backstreet stabbing, I would say even this little was enough, this was light and transformation. It made me hate my life. All hate your lives and change the world!

Scene Two

THE DUKE, THE CARDINAL, *observing.*

DUKE: She is so old...

CARDINAL: Gone forty, yes...

DUKE: I think our officers, however lowly, ought not to scandalize us with weird appetites. Can't he speak to girls?

CARDINAL: I couldn't say.

DUKE: Bianca was a torment to him.

CARDINAL: Really?

DUKE: She tells me he was done before she started.

CARDINAL: Is that so...

DUKE: Mind you, they all say that, I won't tell you the cuckolds I've heard denigrated...

CARDINAL (*aside*). Stop your philandering, I said. Stop this endless fingering of flesh. I said the public do not like to see this in their governor, but they do! I was wrong there. Profoundly wrong. Who rips the sheets with him, and who was grappled half way down the stairs is all public speculation, keeps the masses warm with itching. It's the entertainment of the modern state and the proper function of an aristocracy! No, carry on, I was wrong to reprimand him! There, church dignitary bows to insatiable appetite of prince... (*He bows.*) There is another sex, however...

DUKE: I have never touched a woman over thirty! Not knowingly. Fifteen is best. They gasp in wonder, don't dare speak, eyes all big, half terror and half vanity!

CARDINAL: I think there is another sex, however...

DUKE: What? I've done it all. (*He turns to* THE CARDINAL.) Is there some posture I've not tried? Some practise of the Arabs you in your dusty library have uncovered? **Banned books!** (*He laughs.*) I assure you this is something I also have researched. Look at me, brother, fifty-five, and no part of a girl's anatomy I'm not versed in. Can place my finger blindfold and make them shudder at a licking.

CARDINAL: Yes, I do not doubt it, though this I think is not to do with posture or with bringing off, but something else.

DUKE: What, then?

CARDINAL: Something which unlocks the discipline of the civil state.

DUKE: Go on.

CARDINAL: Let all the population copulate, seduce daughters, bring out the waywardness of wives, whelps and growls from upper storeys all night long, good, satisfaction and quiescence everywhere, but this might lever up whole pavements and turn the fountains red. (*He walks a little, stops.*) You see, it does not lead to childbirth, which by responsibility, might modulate its strength..

DUKE: Oh, come on, stuff your theological euphemisms, what is it, sodomy?

CARDINAL: I don't know yet...

DUKE: Whatever it may be, I've done it.

CARDINAL: Perhaps, I am celibate, and imagine union more immaculate than actually it is. That two might lock, and in locking, undo whole cliffs of discipline seems to me possible...

DUKE: The fevered fantasy of the deprived. Dear brother, you stick to politics.

CARDINAL: **But it is, you see. It is politics.** (*The* DUKE *looks at him, with contempt. Then returns to his observations.*)

DUKE: He dotes upon her, licks the experience out of her wrinkles. And there are girls tight in their skin on every pavement!

Scene Three

THE WARD's *garden.*

WARD: I do love to be in a garden! To poke my head among the flowers and make my hair a roost for doves! I do! I do! Sing me a song, there's a good bitch. (*He sits.*) Am I nice and tame? I have not been out three weeks for cricket, hunting or the like, have not tumbled headlong off the horse and staggered home all shit and brandy, have I? I am the model husband. Sing him a song, he is an idiot. Do you love your idiot?

ISABELLA: You are not advised to call yourself an idiot or—

WARD: I shall be taken for one! Horror! Stack me in the summerhouse, prop me like a deckchair stiff against the wall, or do you have a better use for it? The summerhouse? By the way your breath smells. And only three weeks on the nuptials! Don't neglect yourself or I may lose my fascination with you.

ISABELLA: What fascination? You mean pinching my arse? Your fascination consists entirely in pulling up my skirt and whooping.

WARD: Yes, it does and all! I am an idiot! Lock me in the summerhouse! Or do you have another use for it? I do miss Sordido! I love the doves, I love the clematis, but Sordido was good to sit with in a storm and watch the lightning. I do think sitting with your legs apart is not the way to charm me. I mention it in passing.

ISABELLA: Oh, he cares for my legs, how they face the world!

WARD: I'm not the world, beloved...

ISABELLA: I don't require you stay by me. Please, to your clubs and bars by all means.

WARD: No, no! A man who marries must enjoy the woman not only in the night but in all the glitter of her personality! Is it tedious to be married to an idiot?

ISABELLA (*darkly*). I am not married to one.

WARD (*dark in turn*). No, indeed, but the wife of...? [He *stares at her, and suddenly, clowns*) Catstick! Catstick! (*He stops again.*) I think it is a dirty world, where we are stuck together by some senile whim which thinks our youth will match their sentiments, and our fucking lubricate their arid transactions. (*She looks at him, amazed.*) **Catstick! Catstick!** (*He shudders.*) I do not like you, you are full of grimy sweetness, like a toffee left in pockets...

ISABELLA: You do not need to be the child to me. The fat boy. Do you? You do not...

WARD: Show us yer bum, do! (*She turns, goes out.*) I find my only comfort in the mocking of their shallow ardours. I could no more dance attention on these frills and bustles than shove my hand straight to the wet mouth of their hips, **I do like women with a terrible liking but they are not actual, are they?** (*He pretends to recall.*) Went down to the river with Sordido once, out of the city in the summer and saw a woman on the bank who looked—in simple cloth dress— looked at me, and I hung there, hung back until she wound me in with her desire like something on a hook, closer and closer I went, wordless to her lips, by the washing basket and the scrubbing brush, she found me straight and I found her, no diversion, up to her heart I reached while Sordido lit a pipe beneath the tree and at the finish she went shh, finger to the lips as if words or gratitude would spoil it, as if to speak would bring sin to its purity.... (*Pause*) True story... (*Pause.*) **True like fuck it is.** (*He roars with contemptuous laugher.* SORDIDO *bounds in.*)

SORDIDO: She hurries to her uncle, why?

WARD: Her uncle, why?

SORDIDO: I can't think why!

WARD/SORDIDO: **Oh, why, oh, why!** (*They jerk their pelvises in a ritual.*)

WARD (*embracing him*). I have missed you! I can say in utter honesty, in prefect truth, in sworn and honourable veracity so help me God I longed for your foul observations, did I not!

SORDIDO: Truth? Truth? A perfect truth, what's that?

WARD (*pointing to the floor*). **Saw one!**

SORDIDO: Truth, oi!

WARD (*diving*). Caught it! Down you bugger!

SORDIDO: Net! Net!

WARD: Slippery... slippery...

SORDIDO (*pretending to grapple with invisibility*). Says— says—

WARD (*cupping his ear*). What?

SORDIDO: Squeaks... **Nice—place—you—got.** (*He releases it.*)

WARD: She brought money. She brought flesh. With one tit in my paw I glance across the garden which is designed according to my whim, shape of the dollar enclosing female lip, the box tree is the dollar and the geraniums the lip, and I think where is my mate, his squalid den? And lo, he bounds into my presence. I hate all, and the more I have, the more I hate, old men especially, them I would kill. Women less, they are farcical merely. The duke prods bossy virgins and they think, bliss, oh, bliss, **what is bliss exactly?** I thought of hanging myself with a tennis net, to carry my act to the end, my funeral would be the gladdest event in the social calendar ... (SORDIDO *puts his arm around him.*) Shall we do a murder? Shall we strangle Isabella, or the uncle, in some shuddering copulation up against the summerhouse? That appeals to me, but no, it would be taken as a vengeance, as if I cared who shagged her place! I have not entered her, but laid beside her, irritatingly. Have you yet?

SORDIDO: What?

WARD: Been with a woman?

SORDIDO: Never, as you know.

WARD: Explains their hunger of you, as if by restraint some unknown power's gathered in your parts. It's cruelty! You being rather dirty and rather handsome, two things they stir for in collaboration, they almost whimper as you pass **what is bliss** it's murder, surely?

SORDIDO: Here comes all we loathe, and all we loathe in its company ...

FABRITIO: Good news! Good news!

WARD: 'O says yer can waddle in my garden! (GUARDIANO *and* FABRITIO *enter.* THE WARD *bows a mocking greeting.*) Hatred of age ... Hatred of age ...

FABRITIO: Good news!

WARD: You don't have a key, do you? Walking in on us, I might be in your daughter's frills and then what? Tact! Tact! Under the meandering bees, sticky fingered and arse-rampant! Tact! Tact!

FABRITIO (*wounded*). You were less coarse-spoken prior to the matrimonial ...

WARD: I was less used. I find stacks of vocabulary in my humiliation. Well, humiliation they call it who know me not, among them I count you, beloved guardian, who spent my loot and in cruel boarding houses got me off your back, and you believed my school report I was the dunce!

GUARDIANO: You were! It said so! And you behaved it well enough!

WARD: A proper love would see through a malicious schoolboy's pain.

GUARDIANO: I had such business to attend to I—

WARD: **Catstick!**

GUARDIANO: The responsibilities of the estate—

WARD: **Cat—stick!** (*Pause.* GUARDIANO *concedes.*) My dead parent who enabled me this prettiness the Turks strung across a rigging, tongue out, guts out, genitalia ripped up by the roots, most appropriate, Christian trader, Christian money-hunter, would have swopped his bowel for a dollar, but must admire them, the spirit of adventure, **spirit of adventure it was avarice,** for coming home and buying cunt in furs, this man knows adventure—(*He indicates* SORDIDO.) this is the great adverturer, who never strays from Florence and her gutters, this is the great explorer, the immaculate cartographer of human vice, stuff your funny tribes and exotic animals, your zoos and exhibitions, **all beasts live in Florence, I know, they clamber on my back.** (*He nudges* SORDIDO.) Described your fauna, you know them best.

SORDIDO (*examining* FABRITIO *and* GUARDIANO). Here, for your inspection, two common specimens, adult and mature, in plumage of the mating season—

GUARDIANO: I do not see why we—

WARD: **Respect his genius.**

GUARDIANO: Should be subjected to—

WARD: **His genius. His wit.** (*Pause.* GUARDIANO *acts patience.*)

SORDIDO: The mating season which is not a season but is permanent, stamping their webbed feet on the ground as signal of peculiar distress make calls thus, 'My dignity! My dignity!', a somewhat ugly cry and beaks a-quiver with olfactory obsession with tail feathers of the female. Relation to the European magpie, pica pica, has huge appetite for silver, with which it lines its rather squalid nest, and flocks about midday to the exchange, making the repeated call of 'cash, cash, cash!' until with the onset of the feeding hour, which occupies all afternoon, it makes its graceless flight to overstocked barns leaking dung—

GUARDIANO: All right, all right—

SORDIDO: Most unedifying spectacle, the life cycle of this parasitic bird—

GUARDIANO: Childish—

FABRITIO: Infantile—

GUARDIANO: Repetition of stale ideology... (*He walks a little way, then pointedly.*) What a beautiful garden...

GUARDIANO (*embracing* SORDIDO). He knows everything, and has not strolled beyond the river... what brings you here? And what's bliss, I long to know...

FABRITIO: You have bliss in your bedroom if I know it.

WARD: What, my wife? He calls bliss a body? They know nothing, this ornithology!

FABRITIO: I'll rescue her, she'll not stay with a fiend like you who tricked us playing idiot—(THE WARD *feints to butt him.*) Hit me! Dare you? Hit me?

WARD: No, I shan't crack your eggshell, vain old sparrow, shan't give you the satisfaction, though to strike old men is not offensive to my values...

WARD: We'll end our visit here, and tell you plain and dry what should have been cause for celebration. The Duchess of Florence, soon to be, has chosen your abused young wife as maid at her wedding. Now, you see, a great honour we thought to bring with love you've wrecked with spite and barracking.

FABRITIO (*in angry tears*). Yes, knife-mouth! And she'll not lie with you if I'm her father!

SORDIDO: He don't in any case, except to pinch her bum when she is sleeping. Now, buzz!

He swings a kick at FABRITIO, *and follows them off menacingly.* ISABELLA *appears from cover, staring after them.*

ISABELLA: Peculiar parenthood, that gladly sells me to an idiot, but finding he has mind, is all a-scuttle to rescue me... (*She turns to* THE WARD.) Talk to me...

WARD: Never.

ISABELLA: Lie with me, then. Now, in the sunshine, throw the window open and turn back the sheet. Tell. Do tell.

Scene Four

The Palace. THE MOTHER *and* BIANCA.

MOTHER: I was a widow, having been the good wife to a man not very passionate. Loyal, though not without temptation.

For forty years bred children and clean shirts. Pride in polish. Honour in starch. And now, on the rim of the grave I see—**the riot of lost possibilities!** (*She weeps.*) Oh, roll back the hours, toss off the years! Give me my luscious breasts back, I was robbed...

BIANCA: You have your compensations, surely? Though I can't lay words to them.

MOTHER: Oh shut up, you well-fucked thing. All I can draw to me are scabby, legless soldiers and they would dare to call me hag...

BIANCA: Tell you what! On your grave I'll have inscribed the one word **Honesty.** How's that?

MOTHER: Arrogant bitch.

BIANCA: No! I'll have the mason chip **she cooked for five.** How's that?

MOTHER: Mock on, juvenile, your eyes won't pull forever...

BIANCA: Or better still, **here lay the cleanest carpet in all Florence.**

MOTHER: Piss.

BIANCA: I wound you only to endorse myself. The little conscience lurked, did most certainly, until your son abused me. Then I saw, under his charm lay hatred. Undo the rope of love just once and like a sack of dead and rancid cats all stench pours over your knees and feet. I think men do not like us, though they sweat with wanting, or if they like us, can't fuck except with jogging fondness. No love without hate. That's my discovery to date. Correct me if I'm wrong. Does that accord with your experience?

MOTHER: How would I know... Rather a punch in a sodden bedroom than what I got.

DUKE (*entering*). Oh, your best friend weeping!

MOTHER: Yes, for all the phantoms she would not embrace.

DUKE: I'm not a phantom, embrace me!

MOTHER: I dare not, for some smothered feeling might uncoil...

DUKE: God forbid!

MOTHER (*to* BIANCA). Kiss him, do, I bow down to your ambition... my idiot boy would have worked all hours to get you half a knicker you now toss to the servants from a single wearing... fondle her, she is perfect, she is ruthless, more so than you...

DUKE: And she cannot get enough of me!

MOTHER: Today...

BIANCA: Yes, I am mad for him, and it's not to do with dresses, nor with dinners neither—

MOTHER: No, no...!

BIANCA: It's not! He draws me, look at him. He is a manly man, who makes a woman proud, and after, weak. Strong to be loved by him, and a puddle for his desires...

MOTHER: Excellent. And yet he's ugly! Begging your indulgence. By all we thought in my day. But so what? He's ugly.

DUKE: I am not ugly. I am the Duke.

MOTHER: He is the Duke.

DUKE: No duke is ugly. I could go like the lice-infested tramp, all fingers in the arm pits, and assure you, all the blades would call it fashion and go scratching likewise, and all women would say, how well he scratches, he is the essence of manhood!

BIANCA (*crossly*). It is not so!

DUKE (*placatory*). No, no, indeed...

BIANCA: You humble your fineness, you—(HIPPOLITO *enters. She turns to him, bewildered.*) It is not so, surely, that—he is worth five mundane husbands, surely?

HIPPOLITO: Ten, if yours is fit to go by.

MOTHER: How does he go, my old discarded boy? Often at his castle? He don't invite me ever.

HIPPOLITO: My sister is a fool for him. They carry their joint lechery into the street when they snatch time from the bedroom.

DUKE (*mocking*). In the street! That you would never do! No, sir, discretion is your prime quality.

HIPPOLITO: I do my best.

DUKE: Who would know, to look at him, his neck had travelled through his niece's skirts? Not me, sir!

HIPPOLITO: I'm sorry you find something comical in caution. I shall enjoy my treasure without taking her against the alley wall.

DUKE: Wall-fucking! And the woman is forty!

HIPPOLITO: I think we understand, notionally at least, the power of the oligarchy rests on respect—

DUKE: Respect, is it?

HIPPOLITO: Respect, yes, which is not wall-fucking, is it?

BIANCA: They are in love...

HIPPOLITO: Me, too. But if all love to be believed must entail straddling in public—

DUKE: **Respect? Respect?** Nay, stuff respect. It's violence. Pageantry and violence.

HIPPOLITO:You phrase it nakedly.

DUKE: Why not? I tell you how we govern. Tinsel to the nostrils and a spike at the arse. (HIPPOLITO *bows.*) He looks affronted! Oh, the tasteful man, and he reads books! Hippolito is chock with wisdom, and when he dies, will do it quietly, as he fucks, secure in the knowledge all he did was done with taste and judgement, never coarse and never loud... (*He entertains.*) It is not fair! Is it? Not fair! Some men succeed at everything! I have a mind to glance at Isabella. Where does he keep his clandestine wife?

BIANCA: You dare go sniffing at her skirt—

DUKE: A mind, I said, I have a mind—

BIANCA: Great bastard, I would hack thy organ—(*She advances on him.*)

MOTHER: I think, seeing the way they go on here, it was a simple crew down at the tavern, and I thought them gross when they swore fuck...no, they had no evil such as yours.

DUKE: Drivel, they merely lacked the leisure to refine their lust. Hippolito, you be best man at my marriage.

HIPPOLITO: I thank you, that great honour.

DUKE: And help pay for it!

HIPPOLITO: I thank you for that honour also.

DUKE: He thanks me all the time. All this gratitude, first sign of treason.

HIPPOLITO: Never. I'm of your party.

DUKE: Of it? Squire, you made it! We were shit but one decade ago, forever in the courts of bankruptcy! Now kiss me, and don't get murdered by the opposition. (HIPPOLITO *kisses his cheek.*) My popularity was never higher, and she dangles from me, flashing like some encrusted gem, blinding discontent and dazzling the cynic. Duchess of Florence! How does the title please you?

BIANCA: It enhances my beauty.

DUKE: It does so, and your enhanced beauty in turn enhances me. It would not have troubled me were you a laundress with eight bastards, I would have carried you here. I must have beauty.

MOTHER: Yes, but what is it, this thing beauty?

DUKE: What it is I couldn't tell you. What it is not I know when I look at you.

MOTHER: She has a straight nose, and last year curved noses

were in...

DUKE (*stung*). Stuff your wisdom. I'll tell you what beauty is, it is what all men collude in desiring, and what all men desire I must have, and fuck it, so there, silence your curiosity with that. (BIANCA *looks at him reproachfully*.) She forces crudity out of me, and now I am embarrassed, why do you keep her here? (*He turns to* MOTHER.) You will see, old mother, that the dossers will applaud my wedding and go home warmer than they would be from a meal, there is great nourishment in pageantry. Later, the royal birth will have them gasping who cannot conceive themselves, and those that can will name their stinking brats after ours immaculate... (*He goes to* BIANCA.) Why has she not conceived already, she might grow a belly from a kiss so sweet is her saliva and so fecund her red mouth... (*They gaze at one another*.)

HIPPOLITO: I'll come back later for the details of the wedding...

MOTHER: Be off and leave us... I could watch for hours, like staring at a living picture book... (THE CARDINAL *enters, and watches*.)

CARDINAL: The service says, which I have recited over the bowed heads of the betrothed a thousand times and always wondered at it, 'with my body I thee worship'. What says the Almighty to this other faith? Is he not a jealous god? What worship is it? Can you tell?

MOTHER: Shh!

CARDINAL: It is comprehensible, I do insist!

BIANCA (*Detaching herself*). You would have scientists put microscopes to women's breasts and weigh them in the scales and come out only with the circumference or gravity, not one smatter wiser why it drives a prince to melancholic death he cannot touch them. Mystery! Adore it! There is little enough and it eases my journey through this puddle of dead dreams to know a man might murder for me, just as when I grow loose on my skeleton like her, to know no man will spare me half a glance will help me say, so, time I quit, and make death easy.

DUKE: Hooray! She owns all the words, and all the juices, marvel at her, moist and brilliant bitch, she cuts the air with phrases, then seduces it!

CARDINAL: She is most philosophical for seventeen...

BIANCA: No, I only repeat what clergy tell me, that we all

swill in sin. I have trod by beggars and thought, not, oh, charity, oh, alms, but oh, fragility of consciousness, give me a man who finds me in all this horror—divine!

Scene Five

The street. LIVIA.

LIVIA (*gazing about her*). This hogheap. This ratpile. This dosserdom. The hand goes from mouth, to genital, to arse. Fill, rub, and wipe. The geometry of servile continuation. And yet—in all of them I think the possibility of ridiculing the meanness of God's gift, of yelling to his paucity, I chuck off the three points of my loneliness, I will not be animal but ecstasy!

HIPPOLITO (*entering, taking her roughly by the arm*). There you are, come off the alley—

LIVIA: Don't handle me, I am lecturing the universe—

HIPPOLITO: You expose the madness in yourself, you were better plotting liaisons in the parlour.

LIVIA: Well, I fixed you up, how is your fingering? I will not flatter it by a better title—**you hurt.**

HIPPOLITO: What are you to criticize? You know nothing of our passage.

LIVIA: I do. I see you are the man you were. Therefore your love is drivel.

HIPPOLITO: I loathe your arrogance—your breast is out!

LIVIA: It is ...! Don't dare replace it, or cover the adored and worshipped thing. It fills him with wonder, for all its papery and worn contour, see, it reads you its history, it is no girl's balloon.

HIPPOLITO: Madness! You have come apart somewhere—

LIVIA: Well, yes, all over!

HIPPOLITO: I need but a pair of signatures and you can be transported to a high and ventilated room where nuns will rope you to a bed. I need but two doctor's signatures.

LIVIA: A doctor's signature! I think there is nothing cheaper, or more willingly lent to the state. Look, there goes a doctor, hey! This woman has found a proper use for her—down here, sir—write on a paper she has caught some terrible employment for her—down here, sir—**don't say the**

word—it's a thing for making soldiers for the state—(*To* HIPPOLITO.) **If you had known desire you would not look at me like that.** (*Pause.*) Dear brother, I think you are utterly corrupt, as I was once, and if I'm mad, it's only health to be so. I fling off all the junk of sitting rooms that eased me slowly to a sickening retirement. I am utterly alive, and flow where once I rattled dry as straw on saltmarsh, truly...

HIPPOLITO: I do not know you, sister, and wish I did. Those afternoons bathed in the fountain of your wit, you teased all of society, and every hit was centre...

LIVIA: Teased it, yes, but altered it? I would not go to my grave with such an epitaph as this—she had her salon, she had her wit, she had her teacups and her gin. No, I loathe wit, the rattle of dry words and poets licking one another's sisters. I think we lived an elegant and disgusting life.

HIPPOLITO: We? We? I smell him on your clothes!

LIVIA: Yes!

HIPPOLITO (*seizing her again*). I cannot witness this! This rotting of a woman! (*They struggle. SORDIDO appears.*)

SORDIDO: Oi! You gents make too much noise. Get gone. (HIPPOLITO *looks at* SORDIDO, *hesitates, goes.*) Mrs, you are well-loved, I can see it...

LIVIA: Yes, but for most of mankind it renders me comprehensible as a dumb Arab...

SORDIDO: A stranger even, catches it, some signal like the sailors' flags which read 'I come well satisfied...!'

LIVIA: It's true, and who are you, unnecessarily ragged, feigning the artisan? What are you, a graduate in some obscure science? It won't do in this state to parade your education. Learning, like love, is for the sewers.

SORDIDO: It's the sewers that I live in.

LIVIA: When all above is poison, the sweetest things must flourish in old cracks...

SORDIDO (*looking around*). Please, this is the gutter we are standing in and cops all around us dressed as men—(*He performs spontaneously.*) **Long live the Duke! The Duke a wondrous man, adore the duke there! Adore him you bastard! Roll on his nuptials, etcetera!** He has a big cock, did you know it? Shh! I also pretend to be mad.

LIVIA: I like you. You are not innocent.

SORDIDO: I am made for the age. I carry my brains in my fingers and write nothing. All knowledge lies in instinct, the fugitive carries the truth behind his teeth, don't lend me a

book I will be spotted, **man with a book there!** (*He smiles.*)
Now sleep with me, if I have entertained you. This offer
comes exclusive, since I was a man I've done no more than
kiss, and that but faintly...

LIVIA: Entertained me, yes you have, but the other, thanks I
will not.

SORDIDO: Oh, mingey loyalty to some idle cove, I hate that.

LIVIA: Not loyalty, but hunger for one only, that's proper
chastity. I swear nothing to priests or civil servants.

SORDIDO: He has worked wonders on you...

LIVIA: And me on him. I'm not his instrument. And yet I am.

SORDIDO: Unfair world, he muttered ritually...

LIVIA: No democracy in love.

SORDIDO: None, and I'm no democrat. The word stinks like
fish forgotten on the slab. This wedding will drive me to a
murder—(*He performs again.*) **Long live the duke! His charm,
his love of fun! Adore him you mean-minded bastard!** The
more democracy is clapping the more I feel some growl start
here—(*He indicates his stomach*) and all my cheeks aswamp
with bilious acid, swallow, swallow, choke!

LIVIA: It was not arbitrary, your coming across.

SORDIDO: How could it be? In this state we are all linked
who hate, by little quirks and signs, and eyes to eyes direct
when looking down would be collusion with the great
unanimous approval. The word which characterizes everything is **yes** and no is only fit for whispering—(*He grabs a
passer-by by his lapels.*) Say yes!

MAN: Yes...

SORDIDO: He says it! See! (*He turns back to* LIVIA.) You are
a no, or you could not fuck like that... good day...

He bows. LIVIA *goes off.* BIANCA *and* THE MOTHER
appear, indulging a crowd. LEANTIO *also, suddenly from a new
direction.*

LEANTIO: Hide me, sir!

SORDIDO: Turn edgeways then, I'm not broad.

LEANTIO: Hide me and later I'll explain it.

SORDIDO: No, use me do and fuck explanation.

LEANTIO: Is that the duchess of the state?

SORDIDO: In everything but title...

LEANTIO: Hide me!

SORDIDO: I do, I do, but I must breathe out and naturally I
shrink a little... there, I puff up... (*They stare at* BIANCA.)

LEANTIO: She goes—what does she do—tell me—

SORDIDO: Shopping.

LEANTIO: Shopping, why? She needs nothing.

SORDIDO: What's need to do with shopping?

LEANTIO: She forever decks herself out...

SORDIDO: I hear beneath it all she has a body but none's seen it...

LEANTIO: Who says?

SORDIDO: She is a virgin, sir. The paper says so.

LEANTIO: Look! The poor go ahh, go ahh, go ahh... she is pretty, they are poor, she grins and they go ahh...

SORDIDO: The acme of artificiality.

LEANTIO: No, she means it, which is worse... Turn! She comes by here!

SORDIDO: I charge for this, most mobile tree trunk. Forgive me, I must clap, I have my act to think of... (*He applauds* BIANCA, *who smiles, passes.*)

LEANTIO: They simper at her beauty, but what do they think?

SORDIDO (*darkly*). They see her naked in their mind's eye...

LEANTIO: No, they think her pure, they cannot envisage such whiteness on its back and yelping.

SORDIDO (*staring after* BIANCA). You imagine with authority.

LEANTIO: Her love is crude. Is crude, I tell you. (*They watch her depart.*) There, she clears off leaving the rabble disputing in their rags which bonnet suits her best, like fifty popes had sprayed their misery with water... (*He turns to* SORDIDO.) I thank you. I was seeking my mistress who went out only for some oranges...

SORDIDO: I understand your impatience. Was she smooth and clear-eyed, full of pride in body? It stands out miles, this quality...

LEANTIO: Yes. Are you much experienced with women?

SORDIDO: I've slept with none, but I imagine. (*He goes to leave.*)

LEANTIO: Wait, you prince of scrim and flannel... (SORDIDO *turns.*) The hag was my mother, and the duchess was my wife...

SORDIDO: It's an offence to say so. None have had relations with her but the Duke.

LEANTIO: Well, I tease... (*Pause. Their eyes are locked.*)

SORDIDO (*smiling*). I know it. So much loathing could only come from ripped-up love. They say a fool brought her from

Venice and lost her in a week. You are the fool.

LEANTIO: I struggled miserably with the misapprehension she desired me. Desire she did not.

SORDIDO: Desire? Now that I cannot understand. You mean she—no what is it, this desire? Old men will dribble at her wedding, is that it? And bollocky youths make crude eyes, ramming out their arses, is that it? **And Dukes go thump, thump, thump into her belly, is that it!** (LEANTIO *clasps him round the shoulders, laughing.*)

LEANTIO: I think I love you! You hate all, and who else can be trusted but him who hates with such discrimination?

SORDIDO: I am Sordido, and you may find me in odd attics scratching with the dead men, or swallowing fine wines in the horticultural extravaganza known as Isabella's house... (LEANTIO *starts to go.*) Plot with me. (*He stops.*) I shall burst into the wedding and take the impeccable by force. My first and only entrance to the gateway of all life and death. In her washed matrimonial skin, all scented for the state and bishops' twittering, I'll force her. Down on some polished marbles in foams of lace and splitting fabrics I'll fuck her place! (*Pause.*) There, forget I spoke. Only a vision. I am liable to visions. Comes of poverty and weird alcohols... (LEANTIO *is deeply stirred. He looks long into* SORDIDO, *and* SORDIDO *into him.*) Sometime your life comes to you in the street, drops at your feet like birds dead in the frozen winter. Plop! The crux of your life. And you were only out for oranges... (*He lingers, leaves.* LIVIA *hurries in, eating an orange and carrying a bagful.*)

LIVIA: This crowd of gaping gobs has separated us! (*She kisses him.*) The genuflecting poor! And filthy hands applauding riches! Was there ever a spectacle more like to make lovers ashamed of love? I felt like smacking them out of their servility. (*She holds out the bag.*) Oranges. (*He does not take one.*)

LEANTIO: I met a man...

LIVIA: I also! Do take one, they are so sweet!

LEANTIO: And the man chilled me with a dream.

LIVIA: Look, how huge they are!

LEANTIO (*sending the bag flying*). Piss your oranges! (*They roll across the street. Pause.*)

LIVIA: What dream, Leantio? (*He stares.*)

LEANTIO: A dream not fit for telling. (*He takes her arm.*) Let's get to bed and drown evil in perspiration—

LIVIA: Wait.

LEANTIO: Smother me in your hollows—

LIVIA: Wait, I said—

LEANTIO (*turning angrily on her*). Wait, what for! Wait, you who never waits? What is this hanging back, you with your barmy appetite for love, legs ever open for my fist and now won't shift, why! (*Pause.*)

LIVIA: My flesh is not a pond to drown your fears in. (*Pause.*) Desire's truth, Leantio, and compels it speak. All the rest is fucking. Our union is not a place for hiding in, or a sink to vomit temper. (*Pause.*) What dream, and who was he?

LEANTIO: A dream of Bianca raped. On her wedding morning. (*She goes to him, takes his arm.*) I dare not see more of him! He visits Isabella's house, or you discover him in cellars, so he says, which cellars do you think? A man in black and alive with hate. **He made me long for vegeance on the doll who was my wife.** The dying embers of that instinct he fanned with his imagination, let's go . . .!

LIVIA: Find him.

LEANTIO: Find him?

LIVIA: The man who shakes you so. And drag his dream into the daylight . . .

LEANTIO (*staring at her*). What are you? Livia? (*She extends a hand to him. He does not take it.*) Can't . . . walk beside you but . . . can't touch . . . (*She leads off. He follows. As they leave,* THE CARDINAL *appears, watching.*)

CARDINAL: They walk with space between them. The flesh cool and the veins not hammering . . . what's done that? (*He picks up an orange, contemplatively.*) An idea . . .! Oh, God, an idea has come between them! Oh, easy lust or nagging marriage, this we know and manage, but imagination . . .! **Birth of an idea there!**

Scene Six

The fort at Rouens. A party enters.

LIVIA (*mocking*). Here's a fort to terrify an enemy! The walls are thick with ivy and the cannon in the ditch. As for the garrison, it's nettles!

SORDIDO: Attention, nettles!

LIVIA (*to* LEANTIO). I did not know the reach of the Duke's contempt for you until this minute... he might have smacked you for a cuckold, public in the gob, as give you this derogatory honour. Loose stair there!

WARD (*gazing around*). Leantio, exquisite appointment! Where will you pitch your pennant? A peasant has the flagpole for fencing cattle in! (*Laughter.*)

LIVIA: My skirt's his flag, flapping in the foul wind which blows off Florence. Smell, smell that! (*She breathes in, leaning over the parapet.*) Stink of nightclub and brassy odour of the stock exchange!

WARD (*breathing deeply*). Duke's crevices.

SORDIDO: Officers' fart and dying breath of doorman.

LIVIA: Vomit of the debutante.

SORDIDO: Great stench of black-gummed deference.

LEANTIO: Why gather here? Where is the virtue in it? (*He turns away.*)

LIVIA (*staring at the distant city*). Look, the city glows in dusk... throbs with the pulse of money... we stand outside it and with one finger eliminate corruption... (*She holds up a finger before her eyes.*)

LEANTIO: This is a futile picnic, dancing defiance from a distance...

LIVIA (*turning away*). But laugh we must! Must laugh at wit of dukes, who give decrepit forts to men with decent grudges!

SORDIDO: Laugh, yes, because our joke is better.

LEANTIO: What joke? The ruination of Bianca?

LIVIA: Ruination, why? We save her.

LEANTIO: Save her! By rape! Since when was rape salvation?

LIVIA: Leantio, whole cliffs of lies fall down in storms. By this catastrophe she'll grope for knowledge her ambition hides from her. And simultaneously, Sordido's crime will rock the state off its foundations, which is erected on such lies as ducal marriages.

LEANTIO: I've hated her, God knows the length of my loathing, yet I would not have my basest urgings played to—

LIVIA: Oh, he is so decent, forcing down his feelings!

LEANTIO: What did you love me for?

LIVIA: **Your hunger. Not your decency.** (*She holds him passionately.*) What we have found in love doesn't come to clerks with consciences, all 'does this please you' and 'forgive me, does that hurt?' No, but taking, from the depths of unkind longing! We liberate her from herself, and at the same stroke, unleash contempt on all we've come to hate.

LEANTIO: Where is the realism in all this?

LIVIA: **Realism I hate the word.** (*She contains her fury.*) Shall we, who have come to knowledge and own truth, not act on it? Shall we shrivel up in sarcasms, giggling at the satires of the radicals and make content with sympathizing, doling cash to rebels we're too posh to meet? I have thrown my money to the poor while hating charity, and laughed at criminals while hating crime, and now I act! It kills the soul not to exploit an inspiration! (*Pause.*) Oh, I irritate him with my earnestness! Forgive me, I see enthusiasm is only welcome in the bed...

LEANTIO: Enthusiasm? Enthusiasm's madness, or its sister, what's enthusiasm doing here?

LIVIA (*contemptuously*). Leantio, the clerk...! The clerk is showing through the skin...

LEANTIO (*stung*). You hate Bianca and dress up revenge as politics!

LIVIA: Hate her? No, I pity her. It's you who hates.

LEANTIO: Pity? You? Pity's not a quality I'd pin to you.

LIVIA: Pity, yes. Pity her who uses cunt as property, to buy her way up floors of privilege. When Sordido's forced his pain on her she'll learn the thing she sells can just as well be stolen... (*Pause. He paces.*)

LEANTIO: We rob her of her rights...

SORDIDO: Her right to nay. Her right to yea, she can keep that.

LEANTIO (*paces, turns*). This rape—this rape you call deliverance—

SORDIDO: Rape, indeed, and not the first time...

LEANTIO (*turning on* SORDIDO). Who raped her previously, me?

LIVIA: You? Never you. The Duke. With my connivance. I wrapped her for his lust and tied the ribbon, while you sweated in a foreign port.

LEANTIO: It was seduction, though I shudder to imagine, seduction it was, surely—

SORDIDO: **Violation.** (*Pause.*) Violation, yes, which came by wealth and power. And her protesting mouth was stopped, not by a fist, but greed and glamour suffocated it. By her squalid ambition was repulsion choked. And now, against the Duke's degraded appetite, my purity claims access to her ravaged territory. (*Pause.* LEANTIO *stares at him.*)

LEANTIO: It's death.

SORDIDO: I risk death for her privacy. And stealing her toy virginity, all the poor of Florence grab their rights, who had been meant only to swoon with insatiable envy...

WARD: While he, immaculate rebel, among her moist wound intrudes, I'll shout out **oh, exquisite robbery!**

LIVIA (*laughing, embracing* THE WARD). Here comes your wife, delighted with this mossy tower and thinking it a perfect place to picnic!

WARD (*going to intercept her at the top of the steps*). Beloved! The steps are shattered, mind your ankle!

LIVIA: Through her I will arrange Sordido's entry to the palace. Hurry, leave us...! (SORDIDO *and* THE WARD *hasten down.* LIVIA *turns to* LEANTIO.) Who would have thought I might descend to trickery again? Old skills don't die. Sad truth. (*She caresses him.*) And yet, a thing is vile, not in itself, but only in relation to its usage—

LEANTIO: Not so, that's cruel misuse of reason—

LIVIA: **Of course it's so.** (*He turns from her. Pause.*)

LEANTIO: So, this is the infant of our exceptional love... You labour for a child as hideous as this...

LIVIA: You are so precious, who half-killed me with his passion once... (*Pause. She takes his head in her hands.*) Oh, listen, our love plunged through all layers of affection, burst longing, split open desire, struck seams not of comfort but of truth! We humiliate our long adventure if we draw back from its message!

ISABELLA (*entering*). Oh, pretty place!

LIVIA (*disengaging from* LEANTIO). I knew you'd love it! (*She goes to her side.*) Niece, all's well with you if you adore your husband—(*She turns back to* LEANTIO.) Do leave us to speak a little, private thing...! (LEANTIO *goes out.*) He wants to love you, chaste and passionate, it's true! Is he not kind to you, in preparation? Confirm it, he has not for whole weeks teased you.

ISABELLA: No, he has been weird and considerate...

LIVIA: Exactly! His scheme—of such excessive romance I could blush for him—is to marry you at Bianca's wedding!

ISABELLA: Marry me? We are already married!

LIVIA: Oh, that, no, this one he calls proper. It's the way with these leathery cynics to want white weddings and lace underthings who bawl the dirtiest. (*Pause.*)

ISABELLA: Two weddings? One for the mass... one secret...

LIVIA: Yes! And this with consummation! But one thing. He will have Sordido there as witness, then to depart, no more the irritation to your happiness.

ISABELLA: Sordido...

LIVIA: Smuggle him in, as Gentlemen to you. He'll kiss hands and vanish. You'll hear no more from him.

ISABELLA: Dear Aunt—(*She goes to embrace her.* LIVIA *recoils.*)

LIVIA: No, you only wound me with your gratitude, I merely repeat your loved one's own suggestions. Now, downstairs and join them at the barbecue... (ISABELLA *skips away.*) Nothing's lost... for all my travelling in love, through hurricanes of difference... I believe I'm even better at it...

Scene Seven

The Palace. BIANCA *is bridal.*

BIANCA (*posturing at a mirror*). What do you think?

CARDINAL: Think...

BIANCA: To see me thus. Do you think—she is pretty as a doll—she is so pretty she is—scarcely human—or rather, at some point she is naked under that? (*She walks, turns.*) Do you think, she is a confection of femininity, or rather—I would give my life to kiss her arse? I only ask. I have never been a duchess before.

CARDINAL: I think—you are not a woman at all—but a symbol of the state.

BIANCA: You have a wonderful intellect.

CARDINAL: I have lived my life with symbols. I am wearing symbols. I worship them. I finger them before I sleep.

BIANCA: It is a strange way to spend a life, always the thing that isn't, and never the thing that is. I think your head must ache. And not just your head. Ache... ache... (*She hurries to him, anxious, proud.*) Look what I've done! Look at me! Am I not perfect? Say I'm perfect, you who has been since his cradle, celibate, tell me I am perfect!

CARDINAL: In all ways.

BIANCA: I think this is the absolute of joy! And everything hereafter, downhill. After you have anointed us, and all trumpets and all beggars and all cavalry have pranced and wept and bellowed and spat spit and coughed phlegm and shat their dung and splintered glasses and all old women cried for what they never knew and all the ugly railed at what they never were, I shall on the eiderdown, among cracking of braid and tearing taffeta, go down for his lips, and all the power of the state will huddle at my little, florid entrance . . .

CARDINAL: The state made flesh . . .

BIANCA: There you go—symbols again! Still, if it keeps you sane . . . (*He turns to go, bowing.*) You know, I think there must be poverty, if not of life, then mind. Or we could not love ourselves so much . . . (*He goes out. THE MOTHER enters, adoring.*)

MOTHER: You dazzle, darling. Brilliance splashing through my cataracts. If I were a man, I'd say fuck God, why kneel to him, this is perfection. And it is . . . (*She weeps.*)

BIANCA (*holding her*). I am everything, aren't I? I am everything. There must be me, mustn't there? There must be me, or they would all—

SORDIDO: Despair? (*She turns.*)

BIANCA: You mistook your entrance. Chamberlains and ushers in the hall.

ISABELLA (*entering, crossly*). You should not be here!

SORDIDO: No, this is my entrance—

ISABELLA: No, you go—(*She goes to lead him.*)

SORDIDO: **This is my entrance.** (*He advances on* BIANCA.) I am so immaculate for this. I am not some fetid courtier or mortgagee who labels himself Duke by virtue of some thousand hired guards, no, were he even half-legitimate he could not quarrel with my right **I am thirty and pure.** No dirty walls resounded with my roar as I thumped the belly of the prostitute, am I not good for this, and fit to be your mate? You are no virgin, after all, I flatter you with my infatuation . . .

BIANCA (*sensing his intention, to* ISABELLA). Fetch my officer, who stands outside.

SORDIDO: Drag him in by all means, he has no throat to cry alarm.

ISABELLA (*horrified*). **What is this?**

LIVIA (*entering*). I must, who makes dreams come to life, witness the occurrence. Don't call me hypocrite, what I have dealt in I attend right to the finish.

MOTHER (*recognizing her*). Oh, lady, I know you! We played

chess when I was your neighbour!

LIVIA (*her eyes fixed on* BIANCA). Is that so? The moves I don't recall . . .

BIANCA: Why are you here?

LIVIA: Did I not work your seduction by the governor of this place, and now unwork it . . .

BIANCA: You tremble . . . more than me . . .

LIVIA: Yes . . .

BIANCA: Is this my murder, then?

SORDIDO: Shout help and see. As for gasps, I make allowances . . . (*He goes towards her.*)

MOTHER: Oh, fucking Jesus, they are going to throw her in a heap!

BIANCA: Run, then, and save me! (THE MOTHER *staggers towards the door, meeting* LEANTIO.)

MOTHER: Oh, son, I thought you had a fort . . . (*She turns back.*) I won't go, dear. I think they'll throttle me. And I've never seen this done . . .

BIANCA (*to* LIVIA). You are a woman. Intervene!

LIVIA: No, sweet and perfumed thing, we have the same sex, but are not equally women. It's a false sisterhood you seek in me.

BIANCA: Oh, utter vileness to wreck this wedding . . .

SORDIDO: No, this is the proper matrimony! The people marry you! (*He seizes her.*)

LEANTIO: Oh, dear girl wife, who clung to me in perfect innocence, in shadows of her father's wall—

LIVIA: **It is not her.**

LEANTIO: I hate this life which wrings such changes! (*He weeps on* LIVIA.) Give me the lie of innocence, always the lie—

LIVIA: No, life is alteration, the shedding of all things until at death there's no regret, but all's been spent, discard, discard or petrify! (ISABELLA *runs off.*) Stop her!

SORDIDO (*emerging*). Is that love? Is that?

MOTHER: Search me what love is, son . . .

SORDIDO: **I say it is.**

MOTHER: It is, then . . .

SORDIDO (*to* LIVIA). She loves me . . .

LIVIA (*seeing his madness*). Yes . . .

SORDIDO: **Does I say.** (*He looks around.*) She is a miracle, beneath. It was as if I knew her, and always had. I could die now, and not protest . . .

THE DUKE, HIPPOLITO, THE CARDINAL *burst in armed.*

DUKE: Oh, my property! They stamp about my loveliness! Look, her clothes cling round his boots! Die, you thing of shit and sewerage! (*He kills* SORDIDO.) I am defiled! (HIPPOLITO *goes to attack* LIVIA.) Not her! Keep her for torture! Dogs to lick her womb!

ISABELLA: Bianca! Where is Bianca!

DUKE: See to her, I cannot... cannot come near such a pitch of muddy squalor as my bride is now...

CARDINAL: Can she stand? Or is she injured?

DUKE: **I don't know I haven't looked.** (*He sees* LEANTIO.) You, I understand. So when you die I'll think, through all his twitching, as the skin peels off his flesh, he gloats to know he wounded me, his enemy... (*To* LIVIA.) But you, envious and unwomanly, such a refinement of horror as you deserve will tax the most senior torturer's imagination. I'll send to Turkey, or to China, for the pain that suits you best...

LEANTIO: Mother, even you will suffer...

MOTHER: Me? I've got no politics.

CARDINAL: The blind man also feels the storm.

MOTHER: **I only came 'ere for a decent dinner.**

DUKE (*to* ISABELLA, *who is attending* BIANCA). How is she? She must go through with it, or government is mocked. Sentries are fainting in the heat and mobs of dirty unemployed press on one another's backs. She must go through with it!

HIPPOLITO: All who've witnessed this, kill off. And what's not known will start no rumour.

DUKE (*seeing* BIANCA, *staggering*). Oh, my shame and my—

BIANCA (*seeing* SORDIDO's *body*). You stabbed him...

DUKE: **I slew the thief.** (*He extends a hand to her.*) You are not damaged?

BIANCA: Damaged...

DUKE: You seem—ruffled but—not imperfect...

BIANCA: Imperfect— I—(*She shudders, falls into* THE DUKE's *arms.*)

HIPPOLITO: Press her...! Tell her, on her own two feet. Her coach is squealing on its springs and you should be at the cathedral.

BIANCA: NO—

DUKE: Be sweet now, you are not so very—

BIANCA: Not so very, no—

DUKE: Some spirit for her, to bring back colour in her cheeks—look, the bastard scratched her—**powder it!** (*He turns away, in disgust.*)

BIANCA (*as* HIPPOLITO *comes to examine her*). **Don't touch.** (*She fingers the place.*) Why did he? Was I too beautiful for him? I think he would have snapped my spine, my loveliness enraged him so. Did he hate beauty?

LIVIA: Yes, to see it sell itself—

DUKE: **Powder her cheek.** We are too late already—

BIANCA: No. (*Pause. He stares at her.*) No.

DUKE: I would remind you, lovely as you are—

BIANCA: Are? Liar. You mean were.

DUKE: I would remind you, lovely as you—

BIANCA: **Were—**

DUKE: You are not flesh alone but also state, as I am, also **State.**

BIANCA: You did not mention that behind the statues, I thought you then pure male but now I find—

DUKE: **Mention it? You knew it, hypocrite!** The rod that thrust between your skirts was double thick with wealth and treble thick with power, you flowed for it! (*Pause.*)

BIANCA: Yes . . . and that's not love, is it? Is it? (*She looks at* THE CARDINAL.) Oh, what am I, then? When I go—when I tremble for a man, for this man and not for that one, what is it made of, love?

CARDINAL: A discourse on the origins of passion I more than most, would dearly love to hear deliberated, but in the street all Florence wonders what—

BIANCA: Oh, fuck Florence . . . (*She smiles.*) Well, of course, I have . . . (*She goes to* LIVIA.) Dear woman, your eyes are gates damming back the torrents in your soul . . . (LIVIA *holds her.*) I forgive you . . . the selling of me to this merchant of men . . . and I forgive you twice . . . the undoing of my knotted womb which swelled and gushed to base desire . . . (*To* DUKE *etc.*) I'll not act the coronation. (*She holds* LIVIA.)

HIPPOLITO: This is real shit we're plunged in.

DUKE: Shut up.

HIPPOLITO: I tell you, we—

DUKE: Do up your gob, you quivering bastard!

HIPPOLITO: Ridicule can topple empires . . .

DUKE: I do so hate—at moments of the deepest crisis—clever

dicks delivering homilies! (*He walks a little, stops.*) I ask her once again, and if she won't must stab her and say the violator did it. So I'll convert this farce into a tragedy, and win more pity than contempt. I'll be the black-clad mourner of all Europe, and all future cruelty will be explained away by pain.

HIPPOLITO (*in awe*). Oh, God, the brilliance of him...!

CARDINAL (*aghast*). But she—her beauty—she is so—

DUKE: Oh, he trembles at the well of love! On your knees to her spoiled fundament! (*He thrusts* THE CARDINAL *aside.*) Bianca, adored woman and picture of purity, come now and kneel in sight of all and seal our love. (*He extends a hand. Aside to* MOTHER.) Get pins, do up her garments. (*Pause.* BIANCA *does not respond.*) Never mind the love, then. Kneel anyway. (*His hand remains.*) Come on, we had incredible nights and will again. (*Pause. She still refuses.*) **No act that two could do was not attempted by us, What is this!** (*Weeping, he turns to* THE CARDINAL.) Oh, on her funeral my weeping will be real, I shall go naked through the streets behind her coffin...

BIANCA: I must be truthful. In cunt. If nowhere else, then there. For all the lies we carry, and must carry, lies of politics and kindess, the small lie and the big, I don't protest. All the things we handle leave us stained, but there I do want—**futile, pursuit, who knows**—I do want truth. Not hungering for what my father tutored me was male, or nurses giggling at the soldiers' strut, but what my stripped emotion commands me. And him, utterly anonymous on the floor, did break some bond, for if I loved power, and power was my dream of male, he had it, too. **Help me understand my needs.** (*Pause. They stare at her.*)

DUKE: Yes, will do, and work it out at leisure in our villa, dwarfs and maniacs if that's your craving...

BIANCA: Oh, God, I never felt so cold, such a deep cold and so alone... (*She goes to disrobe.*) Get these clinging weapons off me and I'll wander.

DUKE: **Wander? Wander!** Never wander! You have fucked your entrance into politics, never wander more, you are collared for your lust!

CARDINAL: They are frothing in the streets, and turning over toffee apple stalls...

DUKE: Wander, no... (*He puts his hand to his dagger.*) Forgive me, Lord of Governments, who lends His mercy to him stretched between love and responsibility... (*He goes towards* BIANCA.)

LIVIA: Don't kill her for confusing your costume with your sex...

DUKE (*striking her*). **Hate! Hate the knowing woman!** (*He stares at her.*)

HIPPOLITO: Act then... (THE DUKE *turns to* BIANCA.) Act... (*Pause.* LEANTIO *goes to move, but* LIVIA *restrains him.*)

LEANTIO: Oh, my life's love...

HIPPOLITO: Act, or the market will be trampled and money bleed to death...

CARDINAL: I think, if Christ stood here, his wounds would open to hear money made your god...!

HIPPOLITO: **Act!**

DUKE (*touching* BIANCA's *exposed neck*). Oh, this perfect neck all white with cruelty, it rots—all—calculation— Bianca...! (*He slides down her, to his knees, sobbing.*)

HIPPOLITO: Oh, somebody govern! (*He goes to take the dagger from* THE DUKE, *but* THE WARD *enters.*)

WARD: No rush... (*He goes to the body of* SORDIDO.) Beloved, uncharitable thing. If every stab was gob what a roar of derision would thunder out your corpse! **Do you think it hurt him to be killed?** He hated life, it was absurd to him. His sneering lip! He flung words like shards of glass against the flashy whore and schoolgirls blushing with false innocence, monarchs, tramps, all their posturing he slashed. I shall be so alone..

HIPPOLITO (*inspired*). Govern the state.

WARD: Why? You take me for a cynic, and therefore fit to rule? I'd no more force decisions on the rest than throttle babies in their prams, which I considered once, for humour... (*He looks at* LIVIA.) Let her.

HIPPOLITO: Her? She's been seen skirts-up in the alley

WARD: Good. Let her govern. She knows, and she hates money. Let that be your manifesto! **I love and I hate money.** Quote it, publish now!

HIPPOLITO (*pursuing his intuition*). You, for all your mockery, you have the wisdom, think!

WARD: I am too good an actor. I would tell the truth in such a way to make it unbelievable, and then they'd all rejoice to swallow simple lies! No, she is the fittest for a dynasty.

HIPPOLITO (*hurrying away*). Oh, catastrophe!

BIANCA: Is also birth...

CARDINAL: What?

BIANCA: Catastrophe is also birth. Out the ruins crawls the bloody thing, unrecognizable in the ripped rags of former life. Ghastly breaths of unfamiliar air! Like the infant, expelled from the silent womb, screams red its horror, then tastes oxygen. I have to find my life! (*LIVIA goes to embrace her.*) **Don't touch.** (*she freezes.*) Too new to be suffocated by your impulsive sisterhood. I'll bruise. I'll crush in your embrace...

MOTHER (*staggering*). Take me, someone!

LEANTIO: Oh, you waddling bag of rheumatism and sinking flesh, can't you get enough of life? (*THE WARD tugs her away, then stops, seeing ISABELLA.*)

WARD: Isabella? What of you, then? (*She does not reply, but goes to BIANCA, stands by her.*) Isabella? (*She does not reply. He goes out. There is a cacophony of running feet, yells off. THE CARDINAL goes to make his escape.*)

LIVIA (*seeing him*). Get Christ out of your pocket! He knew money strangled love, and love's corpse stifled imagination, and dead imagination was the ground from which more money grew. Money, death, and money! (*He starts to go.*) **Don't go.**

CARDINAL (*turning violently on her*). Love! To hear you speak of love who engineered this agony! **Murder of words.** (*He goes out. LIVIA reaches a hand to LEANTIO.*)

LIVIA: Leantio, down to the street now. And tell the people we have broken lies and tread the pieces. (*He stares at her.*) Leantio... down to the street now and—

LEANTIO: **Stay by her.** (*He looks at BIANCA.*) Must...

BIANCA: I do not want it, Leantio. Little spasm of male pity. Male violence, male pity. The blow. The charity. Get off...!

ISABELLA: Escape, or we shall never!

LIVIA: Rags, tattered trousseau in the alleys, run! (*Suddenly BIANCA strikes LIVIA in the face. LIVIA reels, as does BIANCA from the force of it. Pause.*)

BIANCA: Thank you... (*They stare at one another, then ISABELLA hurries BIANCA away. Pause, LIVIA, LEANTIO apart and still.*)

DUKE: New duke! (*He points to LEANTIO.*) New duchess! (*He points to LIVIA. LIVIA and LEANTIO go to hurry out.*) Don't love...! Don't love...!

PITY IN HISTORY

Pity in History was commissioned by BBC Television, Birmingham, 1982. It was transmitted on 4 July 1985.

CAST

BOYS A Sergeant	PAUL JESSON
SPONGE ⎫	ROGER FROST
SPILLMAN ⎬ Soldiers	PAUL DALTON
SKINNER ⎭	IAN MERCER
APPS	PATRICK FIELD
CROOP Chaplain	ALAN RICKMAN
FACTOR Officer	PATRICK MALAHIDE
MURGATROYD A Cook	IAN MCDIARMID
GAUKROGER A Mason	NORMAN RODWAY
POOL An Apprentice	STEVAN RIMKUS
VENABLES A Widow	ANNA MASSEY

Directed by   SARAH PIA ANDERSON

Scene One

The nave of a cathedral. The slamming of massive doors and a cacophony of voices. MURGATROYD, *a dying man, is singing from his stretcher at full pitch. A squad of* SOLDIERS, *crazed by battle, shout a catechism initiated by a* SERGEANT *to restore discipline.*

MURGATROYD *(to the tune of 'A-roving').* I'm dy-ing, I'm dying, who shot me, was it Private Apps, I'm dy-ing, I'm dy-ing bas-tard mates!

BOYS: Why are we fighting?

SOLDIERS: Because we are right!

BOYS: Why will we win?

SOLDIERS: Because we are stronger!

BOYS: Why are we stronger?

SOLDIERS: Because God's on our side!

MURGATROYD: I can see you, Apps, I watch you. Apps, eyes right to the stretcher, **look, the dead man's eye!**

BOYS: Are we right to be ruthless?

SOLDIERS: It shortens the pain!

MURGATROYD: Whose pain? What do you know about pain, you know nothing about pain, I got the pain, not you!

BOYS: When shall we show mercy?

SOLDIERS: The day we have won!

MURGATROYD: You ain't gonna win, you don't deserve to win, you're all dead men, **I cooked yer breakfast you ungrateful parasites!**

BOYS: And when will it be?

SOLDIERS: As soon as God wills it!

MURGATROYD: I tell you a funny thing about dying—a funny thing about dying—**listen, will yer, it's a dead man talking!** When I die you all die too—it's a fact you disappear the moment I do and serves you right I never liked you, least of all you, Apps, I been trying to poison you for six weeks, **never trust a cook—**

BOYS: Don't look at 'im, Skinner—

MURGATROYD: Don't look at me, Skinner, oh, Skinner, it 'urts, Christ, Skinner . . .!

BOYS: Why do we say that God's on our side? Spillman!

SPILLMAN: Because—

BOYS: **Spillman!**

SPILLMAN: Because the enemy—is degenerate—and worships false idols—

BOYS: Sponge! Why do we say that God's on our side?

SPONGE: Because it says so in Mark 17—

MURGATROYD: Oh, very good, Sponge, you creep, Sponge, you murderer, Sponge, **call Apps!**

BOYS: Who started this war, was it us?

SOLDIERS: It was not!

BOYS: Who did, then?

SOLDIERS: It was them!

MURGATROYD: **Who murdered the cook!**

BOYS: Why did they?

SKINNER: Because of—

BOYS: Not you, Skinner, Apps!

MURGATROYD: Yes, Apps, why did you, you were messing about with your rifle. Apps, and off it went, Apps, that's what the trigger's for, Apps, you daft bugger—

BOYS: What do we fight for?

SOLDIERS: Our honour! Our rights!

MURGATROYD: I want to protest! Is anyone in touch with God? That man! (*He points to the* CHAPLAIN, *as the* SOLDIERS *lower the stretcher to the floor.*) Yes, you! I was standing with the ladle making soup, the salt-box in the left hand and the ladle in the right, and this bullet comes through the canvas, through the tent, no warning, **what's the explanation you know God,** it stands to reason bullets should be deflected from the cooks! Is the sun going down or is it me?

The SOLDIERS *drift away.*

CROOP: Rest now, you have your pain in a perfect cause—for Christ and justice—

MURGATROYD (*grabbing his arm tightly*). **Where's the justice in this mush?**

CROOP: We have, each one of us, our time of coming and our time of going—

MURGATROYD: **Not good enough!**

CROOP: His will is unknowable—

MURGATROYD: **Not good enough, mush!** Where are they going I saw enough of yer when I was king of the bacon! I'll tell yer a story, there was a cook and he 'ad seven children— **correction! Seven orphans!**

CROOP (*standing up*). You make it hard for yourself.

MURGATROYD: 'Ard for you, you mean! And he joined the army to cook the soldiers' breakfasts and to steal a little of their rations **that is accepted practice**—(CROOP *turns away.*) Don't go, ain't I dying quick enough, my most sincere apologies, Murgatroyd, snuff in silence you will depress the spirits of the troops. **Look you are goin' 'ome and I am not, ain't that a bleedin' scandal?** (*He falls back on the stretcher.*)

Scene Two

An apprentice brings a sandwich to a mason.

POOL: A soldier is dying!

GAUKROGER: Rain falls. Dogs bite. Nurses steal. Shall I go on? Where's the pickle?

POOL: There ain't no pickle. The grocer's boarded up and the baker's been arrested.

GAUKROGER: Pity. I fancied some pickle.

POOL: They've piled their rifles on the altar—

GAUKROGER: You call this a sandwich? It's a floorcloth.

POOL: I'm sorry, guvnor, there's a war on—

GAUKROGER (*intimidating*). I'm sorry there's a war on? You come on like that and I'm sorry I will smack your arse—

POOL: I was only—

GAUKROGER: You come on like greengrocers and whores and I'm sorry I will turn you out, I'm sorry you are an apprentice and you'll find pickle when I want it!

POOL: There ain't no pickle. There ain't no shops, only soldiers.

GAUKROGER: Well, I don't make monuments for shop-keepers after this. Let 'em do their own scrolls and epitaphs

for running off with the mustard. I hate grocers and I hate
their daughters.

POOL: Everybody's run, except 'er at the big 'ouse. She won't
move for nobody. 'Let them crucify me on the door' she says.
Will they?

GAUKROGER: She is a passionate woman. More than that I
won't say.

POOL: She says Cromwell's men tear pictures with their teeth.
Do they?

GAUKROGER: They keep telling us the rebels never get
enough to eat. I believe anything, lies especially. Here—
(*He shoves the remnants of the sandwich at* POOL, *gets up to
work.*) And if the soldiers trip you, laugh, and if they cuff
you, thank 'em. See, I teach you everything... (POOL
carries the toolbag. Sounds of MURGATROYD *singing
deliriously.*)

Scene Three

MURGATROYD: I'm not dead, I'm only pre-tendin', I ain't
in pain, it's a joke, God never borrows, 'e's only lend-in', 'e's
a bugger to blokes who've gone broke!

CROOP: Because he blasphemes, Christ scourges him. And
the more he is scourged, the worse he blasphemes. I never
knew a man die so badly, it dishonours the regiment.

FACTOR: You could barely get good morning out of him
once...

MURGATROYD: Christ was on the cross, yer see, Christ was
on the cross, says Christ, I can't stick much more of this, I
been dyin' for eight hours, I should be very grateful if one of
you lot would stick a spear in me—it was a terrible pain, yer
see, it was making him turn against God, so along came this
soldier named Apps, **yes Apps was 'is name, Appsius Appsius,
it's a fact!**

CROOP (*walking*). This is a place full of sin. Do you feel it?

FACTOR: Which sin?

CROOP: The worship of idols. The mocking of the Lord.
Look around you, it is not a place of worship it's a wedding
cake. Dead men's tombs higher than the altar. Vanity
offends Him, pomp makes His wounds bleed. What do you
say?

FACTOR: Christ went into the temple, and threw o̶
    tables of the money-changers. Coins tinkling do̶
    steps . . .

CROOP: Smash it then. Call the soldiers.

FACTOR: They went barmy today, killing the killed seve̶
    times over . . .

CROOP: They were filled with the fury of God.

FACTOR: At lunchtime the only cadaver they'd seen was their
    grandad, by tea-time they'd walked through an acre of
    brains . . .

CROOP: What are you saying?

FACTOR: The sergeants could hardly restrain them. Had
    them drilling and shouting their names . . .

CROOP: Was not Samson furious, and in his fury pure?

FACTOR: Yes, but give them their dinner.

CROOP: Dinner?

FACTOR: And after dinner, discussion. (CROOP *looks
    disappointed.*) Don't fret, Mr Croop, we'll take hammers to
    the screens, and send the noses of the angels flying through
    the glass . . .

GAUKROGER (*with exaggerated unction*). Good battle,
    gentlemen? I understand the casualties were suitably high?
    The effect of cannon fire, I gather, is even more devastating
    than the manufacturers suggest?

CROOP: Who's this?

GAUKROGER: We listened from the tower, I said to Pool, I
    hope this will not be another skirmish, just cuts and grazes,
    then we heard the cannonade and I knew, this was History
    coming over the hill. Gaukroger's the name, I can produce
    any pattern of memorial, in greensand or granite, granite's
    dearer because it has to travel.

FACTOR: What are you?

GAUKROGER: There's a war on and everybody's barmy, so
    I'll make you an offer, name and number, thirty bob, choice
    of biblical verses, half a dollar, crossed swords a tanner—
    crossed swords are cheap because I have at last drummed
    crossed swords into my apprentice—his lettering leaves
    everything to be desired, and his Latin!

FACTOR: We bury the dead on the field.

GAUKROGER: What about an obelisk?

CROOP: God knows their sacrifice.

GAUKROGER: Yes, but man might easily forget. What do
    you say to a twenty-foot pillar with Corinthian caps, or

reclining warrior with toga and shield askant, with swags in the entablatures—Pool, work this out—or simple urn and bas relief of spoils?

POOL: Fifty bob—

GAUKROGER: Fifty bob, plus cheese and pickle ... (*They stare at him coldly.*) Cheese and pickle I can't quote for, under the circumstances of war.

FACTOR: What are you, a craftsman, or a profiteer?

GAUKROGER: How about angels over a sacophagus? No one catches angels' wings like me. I might have groomed the real thing I am so perfect. Ask Pool who is the best angel carver south of Lincoln.

POOL: You are.

GAUKROGER: I am, he says so. There's Bert Catheter of Bristol, but he's arthritic.

CROOP: There will be no monuments. Monuments are finished.

GAUKROGER: Christ, what's in, then? I've trained Pool for redundancy! Quick, boy, go and sign up with a printer. What's in, gents? Bibles? Or a gunsmith, would you recommend? I promised him a trade, I swore it to his mother. Go and carve rifle stocks for left-handed blind men.

CROOP: Do you find something to mock in the army?

GAUKROGER: No, killing must be done or I lose half of my commissions. (*He turns to a nearby tomb.*) Here's a captain of marines got murdered on an island. I did that twenty years back—I was never very good at skulls, not that there's a call for skulls now. Necrophilia's got unfashionable, they all want swag and trophies.

CROOP: This is God's army, and we rinse out all sin ...

GAUKROGER: Amen ...

CROOP: We demolish all pagan ornament—

GAUKROGER: Well, it's only mass production, half of it—

CROOP: You pander to the ostentation of the vulgar. Pack up your hammers and grow potatoes. (*He goes off. Pause.*)

FACTOR: Sometimes History comes into the quiet man's drawing room, and goes barmy in his china ... were you never a soldier?

GAUKROGER: I was spared the indignity of murdering mothers' sons I'd never met. Nor did I make my trousers dirty. Nor run at other men's commands, nor wanted to scream at pimply boys. I admit in this I am obviously abnormal.

FACTOR: You are a contemptuous old man...

GAUKROGER: Don't flatter me, I can't lend you a penny.

FACTOR: Things have to be broken. He says for God. I say for man. You think you carve, but you carve out slavery when you lend dignity to greedy squires.

GAUKROGER: Tell him when he wants to bust my work, I have a heavy mallet... (*Pause. FACTOR looks at him curiously.*)

FACTOR: Why?

GAUKROGER: I bear no grudges and I like to sleep at night. When I die my coffin will be kicked about. Nothing rests, in peace or otherwise, does it? You spend three years on a chancel-screen and twenty yobbos break it. Across the floor the bits go, and end up in a garden. Come another century, some antiquary restores it, lovingly, with brush and ruler, then a cannon brings it down again. Well, only a fool cries at chaos, it's the condition. I foresee nothing, I expect nothing, and because I do an angel's wing near perfect gives it no rights, no more than a lovely woman expects to win forever, down she goes to dust and wrinkle, do I depress you?

FACTOR: Yes. To hear human endeavour so casually dismissed. Yes, that depresses me.

GAUKROGER: Rejoice in a sandwich, I do.

FACTOR (*seeing* POOL): All that's to spare himself. An excuse for spilling skill in trivia.

POOL: Don't listen to what he says. See what he does. Mind you, it's out of date. (*Pause*) So what, it's out of date.

Scene Four

MURGATROYD *against a pillar.*

MURGATROYD: La, la, la, la-la, la! It's all right, leave a dead man alone, that's decent of yer, I appreciate that, yer doin' it for me, of course you are, yer think the sight of all that 'ealth and vigour's only goin' to depress me. **I do think that's bleedin' considerate**—(*He catches sight of someone.*) **What's that! I saw death creepin' round the pillar! Back you bastard**—la, la, la, la-la la! Oh, it's Apps, it's Apps, hopin' for forgiveness! Forgive you? **I will spit my last bit of froth at you and it will poison your life!**

APPS: **Shuddup, will yer!**

MURGATROYD: **I accuse the army of failing to instruct its soldiers 'ow to die!** They teach you 'ow to kill, what about dying, I will raise this with my MP! **Regulations on dying gracefully!**

APPS: Look, I never did it, yer know I never—

MURGATROYD: **You shot me, you hungry liar,** wasn't the bacon salt enough?

APPS (*to* BOYS *who enters*). Why does 'e keep sayin' it was me?

BOYS: He's delirious...

MURGATROYD (*mocking*). He's delirious... He's delirious... say something sensible and they call you delirious, proper sergeant's talk that is, mother, will you light a candle, there's a scratching in the room...

BOYS: See what I mean—

MURGATROYD: **I'm teasin' yer!**

BOYS: Look, John—

MURGATROYD: Don't John me, I'm not John, call me Corpse—

BOYS: John—

MURGATROYD: **Corpse is the name!** (BOYS *turns to go, bitterly.*) You want me to forgive you, 'ow nice if corpse forgives you, everything's smooth, everything's symmetrical, lie down in yer 'ole and let us get on with it, **I don't forgive you, not this corpse, not Cromwell nor the 'ouse of Commons neither? You got my blood on yer!**

FACTOR: Be quiet, and find a little dignity.

MURGATROYD: A little dignity? A little dignity! Have you seen a little dignity? I saw one a minute ago but it disappeared down a crack. **Find a little dignity, you outlandish rascal you!**

FACTOR: Then just be quiet.

MURGATROYD: Is that an order? Come again? Look, you can't control me 'cos you can't punish me! What are you going to do? Take my leave away! **I've lost my leave forever you!** Really, the impertinence of officers, giving dead men orders, it's a frightful habit, I hear they dip their wives by numbers, take yer armour off, you look ridiculous. There was a captain once, who when they took his pips off, his jacket fell to the ground—there was nothing inside, just a shouting jacket, get yer own breakfast, I'm cooking for Christ now.

FACTOR: This is a regiment of honest and God-fearing men—

MURGATROYD: Oh, you don't want to be afraid of God, I know, I'm 'alf way to His bosom, I would rather be with my wife's old tits any day, I shall never see 'em again, oh . . . **I'm so lonely 'ere** . . .

FACTOR (*at his side*). Have I been a good officer to you?

MURGATROYD: You 'ave and you 'aven't . . .

FACTOR: When have I not been?

MURGATROYD: When you were an officer. When you were a man you were all right, for a few seconds before bed. At cocoa time I saw something human, fluttering on the edges of your eyelids . . . what is this place? Is it Heaven? Spare us an afterlife if you lot turn up . . .

FACTOR: We build a new country here, a new freedom, very sweet, out of our labour and your pain . . .

MURGATROYD: Don't tell a dead man about the future. 'ave you got no tact? (FACTOR *rises slowly to his feet.* MURGATROYD's *eyes close, he breathes hard.*)

FACTOR: Remove him to the crypt. We can't have him here, upsetting the soldiers. (BOYS *and* APPS *bend to lift the stretcher.*)

APPS: What is it—what is it like to die?

BOYS: Marvellous in a good cause, rotten in a bad one. Pick up!

APPS: But why, though . . .

BOYS: The question has no answer, and because it has no answer, it is not a question.

APPS: It is a question!

BOYS: No, it is not a question, it's a mood. Real questions have real answers. How do you govern? Who needs a king? Who owns the land? Who owns the river? All you can do is ask real questions, and the moods will sink to the bottom.

Scene Five

Part of the cathedral. CROOP *in a colloquy.*

CROOP When you look around you, what is it you see? (*Pause. They look at one another.*) You see what?

SPILLMAN: Pride.

CROOP: Good. And how expressed?

SPILLMAN: In idols.

CROOP: Yes. And would Christ like it?

SPILLMAN: No. 'e would be furious.

SKINNER: 'e would go barmy. 'e would go on the rampage 'ere.

CROOP: He would say, in pretending to honour me, you honour yourselves, you hypocrites.

SPILLMAN: So 'e would fill our 'earts with anger, an' we could bash away, an' God would say, look, my soldiers bash the temple down, good lads.

CROOP: Honour my troopers who deliver me from sin—

SPILLMAN: Down with vanity an' greed.

CROOP: Good, for we fight Christ's war and carry out His gospels!

SPONGE: 'old on. *(They look at him.)* Sorry. 'old on. *(Pause.)* 'Cos 'e says, chuck the money changers out the temple. 'e tips the tables over, right? (CROOP *looks at him.*) I mean... what's 'e mean, I mean?

CROOP: Christ comes into—

SPONGE: 'old it—sorry—'old it—

SKINNER: Get it out, Mick—

SPONGE: I mean, I feel I wanna bash the 'ouses...

CROOP: It's God who is offended in his house—

SPONGE: No. It's me. *(Pause.)*

SKINNER: Go on.

SPONGE: It's me 'o's offended...

CROOP: We are not at war with property. Only idolatory...

SPONGE: That is idolatory. Ain't it? When we got in the big 'ouse at Harborough, we was 'ot with fighting, an' we broke the winders, an' we got into the rooms, an' I went up these stairs, the stairs that was wider than my mother's 'ouse, an' at the top of the stairs was this room, an' the room looked bigger than a field, an' it was full of bits, like pictures, an' this furniture, an' it was all there, like it was a church, an' I wanted to smash it, an' I smashed it 'cos it was idolatory. Inlaid whatnots, splinterin', an' vain pictures of geezers fifteen foot 'igh, rip under my boot... an' I loved it... I was full of the Lord... I fuckin' was... *(Pause. CROOP looks at him intently.)*

CROOP: Vandal. Not Christ's trooper.

SPONGE: Somethin' was in it... in all that stuff...

CROOP: Property is the basis of all order.

SPONGE: There was somethin' in that stuff—

CROOP: God's soldiers do not spoil—

SPONGE: Worshipped an' precious an' gorgeous stuff—

CROOP: We fight for the rights of property against injudicial kings—

SPONGE: **Shuddup, will yer!** (*Pause, shock.* A WOMAN *is staring at them.*)

VENABLES: They will cut your hands off, and nail them to a tree. Every hand lifted against the King and God. Hand tree. (*She goes off, watched by them.*)

Scene Six

Part of the cathedral. GAUKROGER *is working on a monument of a reclining figure.*

GAUKROGER (*at last*). You're not watching me.

POOL: I was.

GAUKROGER: No, you were looking at me, but not watching.

POOL (*turning away*). What's it matter, anyway?

GAUKROGER (*stopping*). What's it matter? **I turned down twenty boys who would have stuck their eyeballs to the chisel blade to learn things you're so casual of.**

POOL: They're gonna smash it anyway. Boot it, crack and split and scatter it.

GAUKROGER: You have all the sculpture in the world stored in your fingertips if you watch. And if they do not crush your fingers you can make it all again, like the books can be re-written and all the pictures painted over again, unless they murder all the painters, which can't be done because painters are born every minute, unfortunately. I say unfortunately because there's too much talent and it's got cheap.

POOL: Pack up and run, I say.

GAUKROGER: Where to?

POOL: There's other cathedrals.

GAUKROGER: And when they fall, run to another? All the masons will be herded in one place like mad sheep, offering their services to the bishop. Down will come the wages and you will have fifty starving masons instead of one fed. Stick to where you are. This will pass and you'll get an income if you're patient.

POOL: It's a dead trade, Michael.

GAUKROGER: Pass the chisel.

POOL: You 'eard the preacher. There's gonna be a new God now, official. An' dead quacks an' colonels will go straight under the floor. No purbeck. No alabaster. An' your letterin' ain't so blood marvellous, neither.

GAUKROGER: Oh, listen to him! Before the troops got here you were all compliments about my genius.

POOL: Yeah, well...

GAUKROGER: If the cavaliers had done a bit better on the hill, you would have kept your little rosebud shut.

POOL: Everythin's fallin' apart! No one told me this when I signed my papers. I'm eighteen, and everything's slidin'!

GAUKROGER: Because we work in stone we think all things last like granite, like monarchy, like peace, like marriages. But no. One clean blow of the mallet and the air is full of fragments. Look at my old skull, I could step under a falling tile and when I got home find my old wife in bed with a corporal.

POOL: Unlikely, that...

GAUKROGER: Unlikely, he says. You know nothing. Now watch, I turn the chisel on its back to rub the edge off the angle.. (*They work with concentration, seeing* VENABLES *enter.*)

VENABLES: This is hell. This is rubbish. And God is on our side, the priest said so on Sunday. What's He playing at? I refuse to run away. I will not squat on a cartful of carpets and pee in the bushes. I look their cockney soldiers in the face and they know me as a mistress. My eyes say dislodge me if you dare I have ruled this place for five centuries. How is my husband's tomb?

GAUKROGER: The short rations don't help. And I'm never happy on a ladder...

VENABLES: I'm worried this is not the latest look. What are they doing in Rome?

GAUKROGER: I haven't managed to get to Rome lately...

VENABLES: Don't be sarcastic, you've seen the pattern books, surely?

GAUKROGER: The war's jacked everything.

VENABLES (*touching the finished portions*). My husband had meticulous taste...

GAUKROGER: So I gather. I thought the drapery falling over the tabulua rasa was something he's appreciate, and the tassels are the latest in what I understand is known as naturalism...

VENABLES: You aren't Bernini, are you...? *(She fingers a sculptured hand.)*

GAUKROGER: No, I'm not Bernini.

VENABLES: You're Gaukroger...

GAUKROGER: I'm Gaukroger, I can't pretend otherwise...

VENABLES: He loved the marbles, cold as death...

GAUKROGER: You can't get marbles now—

VENABLES: **It's so infuriating not to get what you want!**

GAUKROGER: Yes, it must be, but purbeck's a very nice stone, warm unfortunately... warm as life...

VENABLES: Nice for who?

GAUKROGER: For me, of course, it cuts nicely...

VENABLES: There was an Italian here six months ago, but he fled. You can't blame him, the puritans think all Italians are popes... the war has ruined English art. Look at Van Dyke.

GAUKROGER: Van who?

VENABLES: Are you being clever?

GAUKROGER: I am very sorry that your husband should have been obliged, for shortage of Italians, to have his monument hacked together by me—

VENABLES: Now you're being silly—

GAUKROGER: An English mason without orginality or—

VENABLES: I said you're being silly.

GAUKROGER: Your ladyship mistakes my wit for pride. I have no pride. If you can't eat it, chuck it, that's my motto. All the same, I'm sorry the Flemish went out, I was getting the hang of the symbols.

VENABLES: This will be the biggest monument in Holchester.

GAUKROGER: Sir Henry was the biggest merchant, so that's only logical.

VENABLES: Eighteen feet from the floor to mantel, and forty lines of tribute. Imagine the unveiling! But that's off now. Everything's off for the duration. Fun's off, dignity's off, but at least they cannot maul the silver. The silver's packed and gone to Antwerp.

GAUKROGER: Antwerp's safe this week.

VENABLES: Lady Digby's china was lost in a wreck.

GAUKROGER: The weather's a rebel—still, it pleases the fish...

VENABLES: I think it amuses you.

GAUKROGER: What?

VENABLES: To see order upset. God's mansion a dung heap. Estates full of weeds. Ungathered crops. Etcetera. I think it does.

GAUKROGER: It rains as much as it shines. I meet plenty who curse the rain, but really, it's wasted breath. *(Pause. She examines a carved hand.)*

VENABLES: That is exquisite ... how many hours did it take?

GAUKROGER: How many hours?

VENABLES: Yes. Someone will ask me and I want to say he spent—that many hours—

GAUKROGER: A dozen...

VENABLES *(pausing)*. Good ... *(She turns to go.)*

GAUKROGER: Mrs—*(She stops.)* I have to be paid yet. *(She remains with her back to him.)* The boy has a mother crippled in bed, and if I get nothing, he gets less. I employ the sentimental argument ... to begin with ...

VENABLES: There's a war on.

GAUKROGER: Everyone says that.

VENABLES: Well, isn't there? My cashbox went to Calais.

GAUKROGER: Ah, it's the way with cashboxes, they do slip away. Cash is a very sensitive thing. I must have an advance, though. We talked about that.

VENABLES: Oh, did we?

GAUKROGER: Yes. *(Pause. She turns at last.)*

VENABLES: I thought you were an artist.

GAUKROGER: Ah...

VENABLES: Superior in sensibility. Above all mercenary consideration. Lofty—

GAUKROGER: Thin?

VENABLES: It bewilders me that the mind or eye that can make that—*(She indicates the sculpted hand.)* should make room for the dirty little clockwork of financial gain ... sordid calculations, the rattling of grasp and profit. Really, I am disappointed, but you learn something of human nature every day, don't you? The little shocks, the tiny horrors. It's still good, but you have spoiled it for me, what do you want?

GAUKROGER: Five dishonourable shillings. *(Pause. She looks at him, then dips into her pocket, removes some coins, holds them out.)* Forgive my taint, but could you make it silver? The pre-war copper's gone quite dead.

VENABLES: Five shillings, you said.

GAUKROGER: I did, but—

VENABLES: That's five shillings, rebels or not.

GAUKROGER: No grocer will take it.

VENABLES: Tell them they must. It is treason to refuse the coin of the realm, report them to a magistrate *(She writes in a notebook.)* Five shillings to the mason, paid with thanks. *(She goes out, watched cruelly by POOL.)*

POOL: That's it. *(He chucks down his chisel, leaps off the ladder.)*

GAUKROGER: What is?

POOL: Sod this. Stuff this.

GAUKROGER: Easy...

POOL *(untying his apron)*. Take yer tools back. Make yer own sandwich. Sorry but stuff this.

GAUKROGER *(working on)*. Where are you going?

POOL: Guess.

GAUKROGER: Oh, I can.

POOL: If they'll have me.

GAUKROGER: Oh, they will.

POOL: Do you blame me?

GAUKROGER: What's blame? The word is not my dictionary.

POOL: Yer think I'm a fool? The war's as good as over.

GAUKROGER: Cocks fight in pits. Dogs bite bears. Boys scream on windy hills and cooks die in basements.

POOL: Look, cut the wisdom, will yer? All this stuff, this life stuff. Tell us, do this, or this, will yer? *(Pause. GAUKROGER stops.)*

GAUKROGER: No.

POOL: Why not? *(He looks angrily at GAUKROGER)* **Why not?** *(GAUKROGER is silent. POOL flings down his apron and stalks out)*

Scene Seven

The crypt, silent and dark. MURGATROYD is lying on the stretcher. His eyes open. Pause.

MURGATROYD: I'm dead. *(Pause.)* **Put the light on somebody.** *(He sits bolt upright, stricken with horror.)* Wait a minute. Use yer 'ead. *(He lies down again.)* I am not dead because I 'ave a body. 'ow do I know I 'ave a body? Because it 'urts. **Right!** *(Pause.)* I've been buried alive. Keep calm, keep calm, you've been buried alive—**keep calm you stupid bugger!** *(He sits up again, takes deep breaths.)* I can't be buried alive because there would be no air, and there is air. I know there's air because I'm breathin'—**where in Christ's name am I, then?** *(He lies back again.)* Calm down, calm down, if I'm alive—why can't I see nothing? I can't see nothing. *(He puts his fingers up before his eyes.)* **I'm blind!** *(He sits bolt upright again.)* **I'm blind!** *(He shuts his eyes.)* I'm alive and I'm blind or I'm dead and its 'ell, or it's night and it's cloudy, or maybe I'm dreamin', will somebody 'elp? *(Pause. He opens his eyes. There is a creak of a massive door, and a sound of something dragging over the floor.)* Oh bloody 'ell... it's 'im... it's Death...

Stiff with horror, MURGATROYD *cranes his head to the source of the sound. A figure in a hooded garment is dragging a cumbersome object into the crypt. By the thin light, it is seen to be* VENABLES *with a massive framed painting which she is concealing.* MURGATROYD *lets out a groan. She sees him. Pause.*

VENABLES: Who the bloody hell are you?
MURGATROYD: War dead.
VENABLES: Well, you can't lie around here.
MURGATROYD: Where am I?
VENABLES: None of your business.
MURGATROYD: Come again?
VENABLES: I am not obliged to explain myself to you. You explain yourself to me.
MURGATROYD: I was born in 1620, my mother was a kitchen maid, I never knew my dad, I 'ad three children by two women, one in Christ's eyes, two without, the two without are 'ealthy, the one who 'ad God's blessing died at birth—where did yer say this was? *(He sees the room is stacked with paintings.)*

Scene Eight

GAUKROGER *is visited at work by* FACTOR. *He watches him for a while.*

FACTOR: A boy comes to me. A boy says in his wisdom, everything is upside down now and the only skill worth having is skill with a rifle. I said that makes you a mercenary. Our soldiers fight for a cause. One soldier with a reason is worth three without. The boy says he will study. So we took him. Do you know the boy?

GAUKROGER *(working)*. He got under my feet.

FACTOR: You take things well. No protest. No squeak.

GAUKROGER: Why shouldn't I? His dying wound won't make me wince.

FACTOR: You're angry and you hide it with your chip, chip, chip...

GAUKROGER: If you insist.

FACTOR: You are, though.

GAUKROGER: Well, he could sniff out a dinner. You are taking my light.. (FACTOR *moves considerately. Pause.*)

FACTOR: This is a moral war we fight. We call it God's war on our side.

GAUKROGER: So I gather. They quote Him on the other, too.

FACTOR: And who is He with, in your judgement?

GAUKROGER: Well, idiot, the side that will win, of course. (FACTOR *walks round him and the monument.*) Don't let me keep you. Or are you being shy, and want to take on as my apprentice? It's seven years and ten for ex-soldiers.

FACTOR: Why the penalty?

GAUKROGER: They take three years to forget. Pass the soft-headed hammer. (FACTOR *hands up a tool.*) There, you've done something useful. *(Pause.)*

FACTOR: Why do you do this? Carve honour for courtiers? Run up splendour for dishonest men?

GAUKROGER: The honest men have nothing to pay me with.

FACTOR: It's a lie, this. Bigger than the altar for a lout who spent his life sipping in clubs and tampering with prostitutes.

GAUKROGER: His blood went bad and blew his heart up three times big, and his foot came of with his boot...

FACTOR: Show that, then.

GAUKROGER: It wasn't part of my commission.

FACTOR: His expression is charitable, though he was mean ... his hand is graceful, though it was tight ... his wig is lovely, though his hair was full of lice ...

GAUKROGER: It doesn't look a bit like him, but it has got life ...

FACTOR: A bad art, this ...

GAUKROGER: Why? It tells the truth.

FACTOR: What truth?

GAUKROGER: That he was rich enough to buy my skill, and vain enough to believe his epitaph. He could have bought Bernini, but Bernini wasn't passing, so he bought Gaukroger for fifteen quid.

FACTOR: I was brought up a poor farmer's son, and when he died he got no stone but a hummock in a damp field, with thistle and cowshit for his dignity. Now I have tramped through thirteen battles fighting haw-haw dukes and their retainers and I find you, poor man, chipping vulgar pomp for my oppressors. You understand what I must do. On seeing a lie, a good man stamps on it, or skins it like an onion till the yellow heart is clear to see ... (GAUKROGER *works on for a long time.*)

GAUKROGER: I want to finish the head ... let me finish the head. ...

Scene Nine

The aisle. The SOLDIERS, *bearing sledgehammers, march down, singing.*

SOLDIERS *(to the tune of 'The Girl I Left Behind Me').* Oh, Jesus Christ belongs to us, His words are plain to see, We don't need no arch—bishops crawling on their knees! *(Then, like a chant, to 'Rule Britannia'.)* **Up the republic! The republic will be free! No more bishops and no bleed-in' monarchy!** *(To the first tune.)* Christ is our mate, 'e makes us hate all things vain and i-dle, Stuff the Bishops and the Pope, We'll find 'im in the Bi-ble! *(Reprise)* **Up the republic! the rep-ublic will be free! No more bishops and no bleed-in monarchy!**

Scene Ten

The crypt. Distant sounds of singing and rampage.

MURGATROYD: This ain't 'eaven. I can 'ear Apps. Apps bawlin'. *(He looks at* VENABLES, *who is still.)* This ain't 'eaven. 'O put me down 'ere?

VENABLES: Shut up, you hideous idiot.

MURGATROYD: **Oi! The cook ain't dead! Down 'ere, lads!**

VENABLES *(taking a blade from her skirt).* Be quiet or I will stab you. *(He looks at her.)* I have no qualms about stabbing. Really. None.

MURGATROYD: No, Mrs, I don't think you 'ave . . . *(Sound of destruction above.)*

Scene Eleven

CROOP *presides over an orgy of destruction.*

CROOP: Oh, Jesus, thy servants attack thy prison, tear down the walls of thy incarceration and bring thy mockers into just rebuke! Behold thy servant Apps in ecstasy of Christ relief!

APPS *(swinging a hammer).* 'ow am I doin'?

CROOP: Good work, soldier in Christ!

APPS: Carry on?

CROOP: He commands thee!

SPONGE: Jesus is in me, Mr Croop.

CROOP: This also is a war, this also is a battle!

SPONGE: 'e says to me, all that offends thee, strike it out . . .

CROOP: Make haste, then! Cast down the fortress of hypocrisy!

SPONGE: That's right, then, is it?

CROOP: Oh, when He works in thee, thou knowest it . . .

SPONGE: That's what I thought . . .

CROOP *(proceeding).* Down Jericho, down, the tinsel of thy enemies!

Scene Twelve

Sounds of wreckage. GAUKROGER, *on a ladder, working.*
POOL *enters, in ill-fitting armour. He waits until* GAUKROGER
catches sight of him.

POOL: Them Gothic canopies we spent three months
on—you should see 'em. An' the Tudor screen—I won't tell
yer ... (GAUKROGER *carries on working*) Tomorrow I do
training on twelve-foot pikes. Present pikes! Slope pikes!
Pikes avaunt! (*Pause.*) Then I get on to muskets. Mark V.
Mark VI are waiting for delivery. (*Pause.*) Flint! Flint
primed! Draw powder! (*Pause.*) Double Dutch to you, ain't
it? Then I got religious training. The Soldiers catechism,
pages 1 to 17 ... (*Pause.*) 'ow do yer like me?

GAUKROGER (*looking contemptuously*): I have heard the
sight of uniforms might make a girl's legs wobbly ...

Sound of soldiery entering.

APPS: 'ullo, 'ullo, what 'ave we 'ere?

GAUKROGER: There. Now talking to you, I haven't
finished.

SKINNER: Off the ladder, mush!

APPS: Off the ladder!

GAUKROGER: I wonder if you might consider leaving this,
as I've yet to be paid for it. Everything else I've settled, ate,
drunk and swallowed it.

SPONGE: Get off the ladder.

APPS: Off the ladder.

GAUKROGER: Ah. Appeal falls on deaf ears.

SKINNER: We'll finish it for you. Down you get. (*He descends
a little way, looks at it finally.*)

FACTOR (*entering*). How do they pay you?

GAUKROGER: With money.

FACTOR: (*to the* SOLDIERS). Where do they have it from?

APPS: Money?

FACTOR: Yes, the money for the mason.

SPONGE: From the Labourer!

FACTOR: From the labour of the ploughman, the woodcutter, the milkwoman, the shepherd, the coal digger.
That is how they have their money. Where is the
tomb of the ploughman, the woodcutter, the milkwoman,
the mason? The place the thief lies dead in is better than his
labourer's house.

GAUKROGER *(turning)*. I shall be in the taproom of the Green Man if any of you want new monuments...

FACTOR: We have no monuments because we worship no one.

GAUKROGER: Then I'll rot in the pub and be buried under the floorboards.

SPONGE: Ol' geezer, we are breakin' it...

GAUKROGER: I'd be glad if you don't steal my hammers, you can trade a decent hammer for a pint—

POOL: **Don't walk out.** *(Pause. He stops.)* **You just made that.**

GAUKROGER: I had a nightmare once. That people spent their lives making something they called Museum. And I went through the door of Museum, and saw great galleries of objects under glass. And I saw my own work, and men were polishing it with soft cloths, and a boy who tried to carve his initials on the tomb was beaten and called delinquent. And Museum grew, until it covered England. Now, let me go.

POOL: **Stay and argue for it.**

GAUKROGER: The plough will go through every palace and the bomb in every bedroom—

POOL: **Codswallop.** *(Pause)* Say what it is. *(Pause.)*

GAUKROGER *(starting to go)*. No pity in History—

POOL: **No. Argue for it.** *(Pause.)* **What is it? Rock, is it?**

FACTOR: It's sweat, and suffering, and going without, and touching caps, and bending knees, and dirty childbirths on old straw, and drinking unclean water and all old England's lovely parks and stinking hospitals...

SPONGE: **Bust it!**

POOL: It's somethin' else—it **is**— *(He turns to GAUKROGER in pain.)* **What is it?** *(Pause.)* Say what it is. It's **you**. Say it. **Say it.** *(Pause.)*

SPONGE *(picking the hammer)*. You do it.

POOL *(Thrusting his face near GAUKROGER's)*: **Why don't you?**

GAUKROGER: Your breath smells of pickle. You've been hiding it.

Pause, then with exasperation POOL grabs the hammer from SPONGE and to a ragged cheer, sets about the monument. GAUKROGER turns to leave.

FACTOR *(standing aside)*. Go on. And think in a quiet place why we could not tolerate the praise of robbery...

(GAUKROGER *hesitates, then leaves.* CROOP *appears at* FACTOR's *side*)

CROOP: What are you saying?

FACTOR: I said we—

CROOP: Yes, I know what you said, I wonder what you are saying... I find the soldiers are less vehement for Christ than grudging against property. I wonder why. I wonder who presumes to teach them. Not me. I teach idolatory to be a sin, not property.

FACTOR: Is there any difference, Mr Croop?

CROOP: Oh, come, come...

FACTOR: Christ teaches—

CROOP: Does He? Are you telling me what Christ teaches? I thought I was the preacher. I thought you were in the artillery.

FACTOR: I quote scripture.

CROOP: Very good. But anyone can quote scripture. I quote scripture myself. The monarchists quote scripture. I don't think there's much future in that.

FACTOR: We fight for Christ's kingdom on earth.

CROOP: You see, saying things like that really doesn't help, does it? I mean, I know what I mean by it, and they know what they mean by it—But what do you mean by it?

FACTOR: I mean there shall be no rich men nor poor men. No leaders and no followers. No vicars and no flocks. *(Pause.)*

CROOP: Yes, I rather thought you did... You are probably aware there is a prohibition against the teaching of communism in the army. Well, of course you do, you are an officer. If anyone can read the Standing Orders it must be you.

FACTOR: This is a civil war, Mr Croop. The longer it goes on, the less civil it gets. Banners fray, and slogans crack, and men who went out simple to the field come back educated, puzzling their wives...

CROOP: Are there many like you in this regiment? *(Pause.)* I ask because... well, I simply ask... (FACTOR *turns and goes.* CROOP *turns to the disorderly* SOLDIERS.) **Why are we fighting?** *(They look at him, bewildered.)* Why are we fighting? *(They stare blankly.)* Come on, come on...

SPILLMAN: Because we are right!

CROOP: Thank you. And why will we win?

BOYS/SKINNER: Because we are stronger?

BOYS: Wake up, Apps!

CROOP *(calmly, softly).* Why are we stronger?

ALL: **Because God's on our side!** *(Pause, they watch him walk up and down in the rubble.)*

CROOP: I think we've done enough destroying. I think if there is one sin more loathsome than all others it is the sin of excess. I think now we learn patience, tolerance and self-control. I think we say, though we have come from battle rough-handed and clumsy in our boots, we might tread among fine things and yet break none. So the people may say of us, look, the regiment passed by with feet as light as angels, though five hundred marched among fine china, they did not break a single cup... *(They stare at him.)*

Scene Thirteen

The crypt. MURGATROYD *is lying fixed by the sight of* VENABLES *blade. Sound of boots marching.*

MURGATROYD: Can I speak? *(Pause. He reads the title of a massive framed painting against his face.)* 'O's Car-a-vaggio?

VENABLES: They're going... We're safe...

MURGATROYD: **Oi! What about the cooks?** *(Pause. The footsteps grow fainter.)*

VENABLES: Let the cooks bury the cooks...

MURGATROYD: Come again?

VENABLES: Blood comes, and all is quiet again, and up the pictures go, back on the walls...

MURGATROYD: Yup...

VENABLES: Undiminished by the human squalor...

MURGATROYD: Yup...

VENABLES: Rebel, I am going to cut your throat. *(Pause. He looks into her eyes.)* Traitor.

MURGATROYD: No, I was lookin' for a job—

VENABLES: Wrecker.

MURGATROYD: This geezer said—

VENABLES: Anti-Christ.

MURGATROYD: Two bob a week and no danger—well, 'e was wrong there, but then 'e never met Apps, did 'e—

VENABLES: Republican.

MURGATROYD: Why 'ave you gone be'ind me...? *(The*

candle in the lantern goes out.) Put on the light ... *(Pause. It is dark.)* Put on the light ...

Scene Fourteen

The nave, full of fractured masonry. GAUKROGER *is drunkenly tripping and stumbling down the aisle. He sees* VENABLES *in front of him, stops.*

GAUKROGER: Oh, Mrs... I have drunk your currency away... and slashed it down the publican's urinal... He said I might have had nine pints, but the wrong man's head was on the coin...

VENABLES: The vermin broke my dead love's tomb...

GAUKROGER: Vermin, as you say, Vermin and Vermin.

VENABLES: Restore this. Every last bit of it. *(Pause.)*

GAUKROGER: Why?

VENABLES: Why?

GAUKROGER: Yes.

VENABLES: Did you say why?

GAUKROGER: I think I did. Maybe it wasn't me...

VENABLES: **Why, he says. We need great art, that's why.** *(Pause.)* Are you drunk, or acting?

GAUKROGER: I think I could be Bernini.

VENABLES: You are drunk.

GAUKROGER: I think—I think if only I had drunk more—I would have been **a great original**... *(He looks up to her eyes.)* Where's my **tool bag, I am full of visions!** Give the man a drink and let his dreams out of the bottle! There it is, look—*(He belches.)* **Inspiration!** *(He trips, falls among broken stones. He picks one fractured item up.)* Oh, look at that... I could spend ten years and never get a shape as fine as that... I praise this object as evidence that great art is only born of temper! **Let the infantry in the museums!**

VENABLES: I wish to speak to you. Get off the floor.

GAUKROGER: Look how improved all my stale old labour is...

VENABLES: We have to have art or we don't know who we are. It's very simple. Do get up.

GAUKROGER: The crack is better than my line, the accident far better than the carving... *(He holds up a smashed item of sculpture.)* Poor boys who had a little beauty, under their pimples and cropped heads ... how do all my studied scrolls compare with that? **That's life!**

VENABLES: You've gone barmy. Shock or liquor's made you daft.

GAUKROGER: **Don't you see there's life in that!**

VENABLES: When all the world is tilted we need people who can keep their feet, who say of all calamity, this is a setback, but I hold to my own truth, I will not waver. The storm of history. When it has passed, clean up. Stone on stone. Brick on brick.

GAUKROGER (*seeing blood on her dress*): Ladies shouldn't sew. They only prick their fingers ... (*Pause.*) That's cook's stuff on your dress ... the colour of old gravy ... where is he?

VENABLES: **Where is who, silly?**

Scene Fifteen

The crypt, MURGATROYD *lies dead on the bench.* GAUKROGER *is heard singing.*

GAUKROGER: Oh, Mother, do not fret for me/I am not in the infan-try/But round the stew-pot pass the day/Far from the dying and the fray/And sip the rations of the men/Who won't be coming back a—gain .... (GAUKROGER *appears, holding a light.* VENABLES *behind.*) Stand up the dead man! I smell your soup!

VENABLES: Mind the masters!

GAUKROGER: Mind the masters!

VENABLES: Over there ...

GAUKROGER: Master on the right! Where is he? Cook! (*He comes to him.*) Oh, you have two wounds, wasn't one enough for you, you have to be murdered twice, the greed of the unfortunate—(*He goes to lift him.*)

VENABLES: Mind the masters! (*He tries to hoist* MURGATROYD.) Get on my back, you can't stay here, you're no work of art, are you, God's chisel slipped on your phizog, you were made in the evening, nothing beautiful is created after five o'clock ...

VENABLES: Mind the Caravaggio!

GAUKROGER: Caravaggio!

VENABLES: They ran riot in the cathedral, talked sordidly in chapels **but God hid my pictures from their eyes, showing He loves art!**

GAUKROGER: I claim this man's a saint.

VENABLES: Why?

GAUKROGER: Because he loved life so much he wouldn't leave it voluntary. What greater compliment to God? I say the cooks shall sit on the right hand of God and the soldiers shall be thrust into hell. Who murders cooks kills life. Show me a cook with a medal and I'll show you a mason with a mansion.

VENABLES: Dump him where you see fit.

GAUKROGER: I'll stick him with the tatters of a bishop.

VENABLES: No.

GAUKROGER: Why, where's better? Half the tombs have been smashed open. It's a paradise for murderers, this war.

VENABLES: He was an atheist.

GAUKROGER: No man who cursed God half so much could be one.

VENABLES: Oh, very well, do as you wish. *(The mount the steps,* GAUKROGER *carrying the body on his back.)*

Scene Sixteen

As GAUKROGER *staggers down the aisle with* MURGATROYD's *body, the* SERGEANT *steps out from behind a pillar. He taps his thigh with a switch.* GAUKROGER *stops. Pause.*

BOYS: I'm looking for a body. *(The briefest pause.)*

GAUKROGER: Have you tried the churchyard?

BOYS: Done the churchyard.

GAUKROGER: No bodies there?

BOYS: Are you hiding him?

GAUKROGER: Well, now you ask me... *(He turns to* VENABLES, *revealing the entire length of* MURGATROYD's *corpse.)* Am I hiding him?

VENABLES: No...

GAUKROGER *(turning back to* BOYS). She says no.

BOYS: If you see him, we are camping at Ancaster.

GAUKROGER: Ancaster...

BOYS: Tell him to catch up.

GAUKROGER: I will do.

BOYS: No man who has joined can leave us, except by de-mob or death. Tell him.

GAUKROGER: I will do. (*Pause, the* SERGEANT *looks at* GAUKROGER *severely, then turns on his heel. He goes a little way, stops.*)

BOYS: He died, then? The cook?

VENABLES: Yes.

BOYS: We thought he would never...

GAUKROGER: There's no never with death... so far as we know... (BOYS *looks a moment, then goes out. They stare until he is gone.*)

VENABLES: Thank you.

GAUKROGER: Oh, don't thank me.

VENABLES: I must do—I'll write to you from Calais.

GAUKROGER: Oh, don't write to me from Calais! Pay me instead. (*Pause.*)

VENABLES: How much?

GAUKROGER: All of it.

VENABLES: It's busted—

GAUKROGER: Not by me. (*Pause.*)

VENABLES: Robbery!

GAUKROGER (*slyly*): Murder...

VENABLES: When England's back to normal. Come to me, then. All bills will be settled, and loyalties made good... (*She makes to go.*)

GAUKROGER: Will it be long, do you think? I mean before tea-time? (*She looks at him, goes out.* GAUKROGER *lowers the body to the floor. He sits down, leaning against a tomb.*) I carved a hand, and I imagined its destruction. I made love to my wife, and I imagined her an old woman. I ate, and even as I looked at the plate, I imagined myself starving. And now the hand is destroyed, and the old woman is an old woman, and I'm starving. It's no preparation... (*Pause. A hand appears from inside the tomb, holding a sandwich.*)

POOL: Guvnor?

GAUKROGER (*looking at it*). You ass. You have deserted. (*He takes the sandwich and bites into it.* POOL's *face appears in the crack.*)

POOL: I'm sorry I—

GAUKROGER: You'll—get—hung—for this—

POOL: Come again?

GAUKROGER: Changing your mind—they don't allow it.

POOL: I never stole no armour. Put it back.

GAUKROGER: I can't pay you.

POOL: Teach us to do the 'and, Michael. The 'and recumbent. The 'and demonstrative—

GAUKROGER: Dead art.

POOL: Never.

GAUKROGER: Frilly cuffs and whispering Catholics, scented fingers made for intrigues . . . the new hand will have blunt fingers, not made for running up a woman's knee . . .

POOL: We'll get it—

GAUKROGER: **Can't teach you.** *(Pause.)* Can't eat this sandwich, either . . .

POOL *(aghast).* Can't eat a sandwich . . .?

GAUKROGER: Something's sticking round my teeth . . . I think it's History . . .

POOL *(scrambling out the tomb).* **Geddup, Gaukroger!**
(GAUKROGER *shrugs.* POOL *squats before him.)* Find the language. Find the style. New manner for new situation. When in doubt, invent. Copy. Cheat. Get by.

GAUKROGER: He lectures me . . .

POOL: Calamity, all right, bowled over, flat on yer back, looks bad, admitted, but not fatal, still got 'ands, still got 'eyes—

GAUKROGER: He exhorteth me . . .

POOL: **Stick with it, Michael, eh?** *(Pause.* GAUKROGER *looks at him wearily.)*

GAUKROGER: Give us a hand. (POOL *pulls him to his feet.)* Help me put this saint away. (POOL *impulsively kisses* GAUKROGER's *hand.)*

POOL: Sorry.

GAUKROGER: Sorry? Why?

POOL: I know 'ow you 'ate sentiment.

GAUKROGER: Comes of chipping it all day. Like the undertaker, when his wife was dying, pleaded 'Dearly Beloved, Don't Depart!' Too much imitation leaves you nothing for the real . . .

POOL: Was real. (GAUKROGER *embraces* POOL.) Was real . . .